A TEACHER'S GUIDE
TO READING
PIAGET

TEACHER'S GUIDE
TO READING
PIAGET

by
MOLLY BREARLEY
Principal, Froebel Educational Institute

and
ELIZABETH HITCHFIELD
Senior Lecturer, Froebel Educational Institute

Routledge & Kegan Paul
LONDON

First published 1966
by Routledge & Kegan Paul Ltd
Broadway House, 68-74 Carter Lane
London, EC4V 5EL

Reprinted
1967, 1968, 1970 and 1972

Printed in Great Britain by
Redwood Press Limited, Trowbridge, Wiltshire

ISBN 0 7100 1108 3 (c)
ISBN 0 7100 2895 4 (p)

CONTENTS

The authors wish to record their deep appreciation of the vigilant help afforded by Mr. Nathan Isaacs without whom the work would not have been undertaken. They are indebted to him for many discussions and criticisms. In addition there are incorporated into the text a number of minor but illuminating re-translations from the original Piaget works on his advice.

We would like to thank Professor Piaget and Dr. Inhelder for their permission to quote extensively from their works, and for the help they have given us by making constructive criticisms.

PREFACE

IT IS IMPORTANT that practising teachers should read at least some of the works of Piaget which are quoted here since it is only through their efforts that the truths uncovered by his work can be fully implemented in education.

The difficulties in the way of reading these works can often be surmounted by acquiring a *method* of reading them. In our experience a synoptic account of Piaget's ideas is very much more difficult to understand than an account of an experiment followed by a discussion of its theoretical and practical implications. (Piaget himself commonly begins with a theoretical exposition which is complex to follow whereas his examples have a beautiful and detailed clarity and simplicity.) The sequence of presentation we have adopted is analogous to teachers' daily procedure in the classroom where experience must be followed by reflection in order to plan future work.

The writers, having come to some understanding of the work of Piaget by constant reading, discussion and attempted application, decided that some record of their excursions in thought might encourage others to make a way into the material, the implications of

which urgently need to be worked out in the practice
of teaching.

Constant experiment goes on in each classroom so
that each teacher gradually learns, through daily observation of children at work, those laws of child
development which adults must heed if they are to
educate well. There are some people who are naturally keen, quick observers with a special flair for
abstracting what is important, but most people need
guidance and training in observing and assessing
what is observed and this is not accomplished completely in one or even three years of teacher training; it has to be developed through years of experience. Professor Piaget has shown us a technique of
observation which could greatly aid this process and
which can be carried out by anyone living or working with children. This is frequently referred to as
the clinical method neatly summed up by Claparède
as follows:

> 'The clinical method is the art of questioning: it
> does not confine itself to superficial observation, but
> aims at capturing what is hidden behind the im-
> mediate appearance of things. It analyses down to its
> ultimate constituents the least little remark made by
> the child. It does not give up the struggle when the
> child gives incomprehensible answers but only fol-
> lows closer in chase of the ever-receding thought,
> drives it from cover, pursues and tracks it down, till
> it can seize it, dissect it and lay bare the secret of its
> composition'. (Introduction to Language and
> Thought of the Child, J. Piaget, 1926.)

It is not only the fact that Piaget's books have to be
read in translation by most people that makes them

difficult but the ideas themselves are revolutionary in that they seek to explain the child's intellectual life in terms of his own action and its internalisation rather than as the emergence and training of an inherited ability. As Nathan Isaacs says, 'we owe to him a striking fresh picture of the child himself as the main architect of this (intellectual) growth.'

Piaget helps us to see the developmental significance of a child's failures and successes in thought and action during everyday experience by breaking down each activity into its separate mental elements. We have to try to draw the educational implications from the developmental facts thus revealed. In recent years teachers have had to learn a great deal about mental measurement as this has become an important feature in our educational structure. This has led to much emphasis on the quantitative assessment of intellectual ability, since in most intelligence tests the main concern is with the number of right responses. In his 'open-ended tests' Piaget seeks to find in a large number of situations what it is that we take for granted which the children have not grasped. To do this he examines the *processes* of thought and the *degree* of success and failure, which should be of much greater diagnostic value to the practising teacher. It also gives further support to those who believe in the need for an individual approach to each child's learning.

For many years, people who have worked in child centred education have had philosophical theory and intuitive judgment to guide them, but have lacked scientific justification for what they were doing. Piaget's work is now providing scientific evidence from experiments, with concrete examples and demonstration from children's behaviour for what was previously a matter of opinion.

We chose the examples to cover a wide age range partly to emphasise the genetic approach and partly to appeal to as wide an audience of teachers as possible. In addition we tried to choose pieces that held special promise of applicability in schools.

We are aware that our own beliefs about education are likely to have influenced our choice of material and the conclusions we have drawn from it. This has not, however, been the main purpose of the work, nor has it been to save people the trouble of reading the text but to give courage to begin what for most of us is a formidable task.

I

NUMBER

[Extracts from: *'The Child's Conception of Number'* by Jean Piaget (Routledge and Kegan Paul), 1952]

THE SUBJECT OF MATHEMATICS is receiving considerable attention at the present time. It has assumed great importance because we need far more, better-qualified scientists and technicians in our society than we have had before. This demand has brought with it an awareness of the fact that many adults have limited mathematical ability and, what is more serious, unhelpful attitudes to the subject which prevent them from developing further interest and understanding in it. "I can't do maths!" "I've never been any good at numbers!" "If anything involves figures my mind goes a blank!" These are common statements and it would not be difficult to collect hundreds more in the same vein. It has meant that those who are successful in even elementary mathematics are held in some awe as if they had a special gift which set them apart from others. However, it may be simply that they were the lucky ones who were able to make good use of the kind of teaching

1

they received in school. Perhaps other kinds of teaching will develop similar abilities in more people, and at least make it possible for them to feel greater confidence in their power to master the basic concepts of arithmetic, algebra and geometry.

Anyone who is considering the teaching of mathematics must take into account the work of Piaget. He has clearly demonstrated that the formation of sound mathematical concepts depends on the whole previous experience and development of the individual learner, of which particular aspects are successively organised by planned teaching of the logical steps of the subject. It is easy to assume that children are ready to start their learning at the point in a subject at which the teacher chooses to begin, but in fact it is essential to know what particular experiences should have been encountered to prepare them to form the basic concepts of the subject matter involved.

In *The Child's Conception of Number* Piaget traces the development in young children of the processes of thinking which lead to an understanding of number. He sets out a series of ingenious experiments which were performed with children between the ages of four and eight years old. Each experiment presented to a child necessitates his active use of materials, and this is followed up with detailed questions relating to what he has seen or done or commented upon. The results of the experiments and the conversations are then presented under three main headings, Stage I, Stage II and Stage III, describing the reactions and comments of the children.

It is perhaps important to make clear at this point Piaget's uses of the term 'stages'.

A. His fundamental thesis is that intellectual growth takes place in a succession of stages in all children, namely the sensory-motor stage (0-2 yrs), the symbolic-representational stage (up to 5 yrs), growth into the concrete operational stage (5-7 yrs), growth within the concrete operational stage (7-11 yrs), and lastly the growth into the formal operational stage (11 + yrs). (Examples and clarification of these will follow in the text and a summary in the conclusion). It is the order of succession and the fact of the incorporation of each stage into succeeding ones that is important. He is not concerned to establish a rigid relationship between chronological ages and these stages, although he attaches an approximate age range to each.

B. In testing and developing the implications of the above theory Piaget has examined in detail the growth of understanding in particular areas of knowledge, e.g. number, space, time, logic. He uses the word 'stages' again, this time to categorize the children's reactions to specific test situations.

Stage I answers characterize those children who cannot answer the questions, apparently because they do not understand the nature of the task or the principles involved in it, or those who try to answer the questions but show, by their conclusions, that they are not thinking along the same lines as adults.

Stage II—those who are in a transitional phase, groping towards the right solution, sometimes correct, sometimes incorrect in their answers.

Stage III—those who by correct response and explanation can justify their answers and show they have attained a steady understanding of the concepts involved.

We are indebted to Mr. Isaacs for pointing out a possible cause of confusion when reading the different volumes of Piaget's work. Sometimes Stage I represents total ignorance of the task in the experiment (see Ch. IV 'Perspective') and sometimes it represents

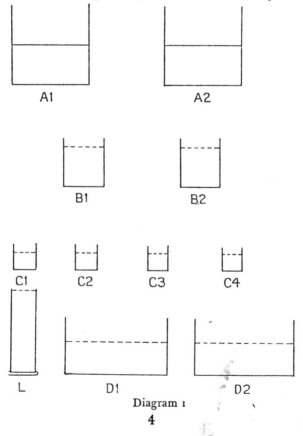

Diagram 1

the condition of understanding the question but not being able to carry out the task. (See Ch. VI 'Floating and Sinking'). Mr. Isaacs suggests that if Stage Zero were used to represent the former state of complete ignorance, this would help to keep more clearly in mind the difference between failure because of lack of verbal understanding and genuine inability to solve a particular problem.

The first chapter in the volume on 'Number' deals with the 'Conservation of Continuous Quantities' (i.e. material that is not composed of separate units. By way of contrast beads are used in a later experiment as an example of discontinuous quantity.) The continuous quantity used in this experiment is liquid. A child is presented with two identical beakers (A1 and A2) that contain exactly the same amount of liquid, which can be checked by inspection. Then the liquid from one beaker is poured into two smaller containers of equal dimensions (B1 and B2). The child is then asked whether the amount of liquid in the two smaller containers is equal to that in the larger beaker. Even smaller containers are introduced (C1, C2, C3, C4) and some of different shapes e.g. L a long and narrow glass and D1, D2, wide, shallow glasses. (See Diagram 1.)

Here is an example of a child whose responses indicate that the quantity of liquid appears to her to increase or diminish according to the shape or the number of containers it is in: —

STAGE I: ABSENCE OF CONSERVATION

"SIM (5; 0). She was shown A1 and A2 half full. 'There's the same amount in the glasses, isn't there?

—(She verified it) *Yes.*—Look, Renée, who has the lemonade, pours it out like this (pouring A_1 into B_1 and B_2, which were thus about $3/5$ full). Have you both still the same amount to drink?—*No. Renée has more because she has two glasses*—What could you do to have the same amount?—*Pour mine into two glasses.* (She poured A_2 into B_3 and B_4.)—Have you both got the same now?—(She looked for a long time at the 4 glasses) *Yes.*—Now Madeleine (herself) is going to pour her two glasses into three (B_3 and B_4 into C_1, C_2 and C_3). Are they the same now?—*No.*—Who has more to drink?—*Madeleine, because she has three glasses. Renée must pour hers too into three glasses.* (Renée's B_1 and B_2 were poured into C_5, C_6 and C_7). There.—*It's the same.* —But now Madeleine pours hers into a fourth glass (C_4, which was filled with a little from C_1, C_2 and C_3). Have you both the same amount?—*I've got more.*—Is there more of the lemonade (C_5, C_6 and C_7) or of the orangeade (C_1, C_2, C_3 and C_4)?—*The orangeade.*—(The two big glasses A_1 and A_2 were then put before her). Look, we're going to pour back all the lemonade into this one (A_1) as it was before, and all the orangeade into that one. Where will the lemonade come up to?—(She indicated a certain level)—and the orangeade?—(She indicated a high level.)—Will the orangeade be higher than the lemonade?—*Yes, there's more orangeade* (pointing to the level she had indicated) *because there's more orangeade here* (pointing to C_1, C_2, C_3 and C_4).— You think it will come up here?—*Yes.*—(This level was marked by an elastic band and she herself poured in the liquid and was delighted to find that it came up to the band. But when she poured the lemonade into A_1 she was very much surprised to find that it reached the same level.) *It's the same!—*

How's that?—*I think we've put a little back, and now it's the same.'*

It is clear that so far the child had thought that there were changes in quantity when the number of glasses varied, but with the next question the level intervenes: 'Look, Madeleine pours the orangeade into that glass (A2 was poured into L, which was longer and narrower. L was then $\frac{3}{4}$ full, whereas the lemonade in A1 came only half way up.)—*There's more orangeade, because it's higher.*—Is there more to drink, or does it just look as if there is?—*There's more to drink.*—And now, pouring the lemonade into B1 and B2 and the orangeade into D1 and D2 which were wide, low glasses)?—*It's the orangeade that's more, because there* (in D1 and D2) *there's a lot.*—So if we pour the lemonade and the orangeade back here (A2 and A1), will the orangeade come up higher or will they be the same?—*Higher.*' She poured D1 and D2 back into A2, and B1 and B2 back into A1, and was again much surprised to see that the levels were the same."

Piaget says of children who give responses similar to Sim that they have not yet formed the notion of the conservation of quantity. Such children obviously know many things about orangeade and lemonade, and if questions were asked about the colour or taste they would no doubt respond correctly; they can even manage the activities of pouring and sharing if the situation is helpful i.e. if containers are the same in size and shape. Where these children go wrong in this experiment is in using inappropriate criteria on which to base their judgments. Their attention is caught by the height or the width or the number of containers and they reason from what they can see i.e. change of shape of container to 'tall' means change of amount of liquid to 'more'. They do not take into account the transformation which has taken place (e.g. from 'wide but not far up' to 'far up but not wide') but reason only on appearance.

The next example is from the record of a child who has gone a step further than Sim. Edi answers correctly that the quantity of liquid remains the same when poured from A into B1 and B2, but when three or more containers are used he gives wrong answers. This is typical of the response of children at Stage II. They give evidence of some awareness of the factors which must be taken into account in the transference of the liquid to different receptacles, but they vacillate between consideration of these factors and the strong influence of their direct perceptions (i.e. what they actually *see*—more jars or a higher level of liquid).

STAGE II: INTERMEDIARY REACTIONS

"EDI (6; 4): 'Is there the same in these two glasses A1 and A2)?—*Yes.*—Your mummy says to you: Instead of giving your milk in this glass (A1), I give it to you in these two (B1 and B2), one in the morning and one at night. (It is poured out.) Where will you have most to drink, here (A2) or there (B1 + B2)?—*It's the same.*—That's right. Now, instead of giving it to you in these two (B1 and B2), she gives it to you in three (pouring A2 into C1, C2 and C3), one in the morning, one at lunch-time and one at night. Is it the same in two as in the three, or not?—*It's the same in 3 as in 2 . . . No, in 3 there's more.*—Why?— . . .—(B1 and B2 were poured back into A1.) and if you pour the three (C1 + C2 + C3) back into that one (A2) how far up will it come?—(He pointed to a level higher than that in A1.)—And if we pour these 3 into 4 glasses (doing so into $C_1 + C_2 + C_3 + C_4$, with a consequent lowering of the level) and then pour it all back into the big one (A2), how far up will it come?—(He pointed to a still higher level.) —And with 5?—(He showed a still higher level.)— And with 6?—*There wouldn't be enough room in the glass.'* "

Finally there are children like Bert who can assume conservation of quantity throughout the experiments. His replies are characteristic of children at Stage III. They answer quickly and confidently and can add a logical justification to support their judgments.

STAGE III: NECESSARY CONSERVATION

"BERT (7; 2): 'The orangeade (A1, $\frac{2}{3}$ full) is for Jacqueline, the lemonade (A2, $\frac{1}{2}$ full) is for you. Who has more?—*Jacqueline.*—You pour yours (A2) into these two (B1 + B2, which were then full). Who has more?—*It's still Jacqueline.*—Why?—*Because she has more.*—And if you pour this (B1) into those (C1 + C2)?—*It's still Jacqueline, because she has a lot.*—Every change produced the same result: *It's Jacqueline, because I saw before that she had more.* Then A3, equal to A4, was poured into C1 + C2: *It's still the same, because I saw before in the other glass that it was the same.*—But how can it still be the same?—*You empty it and put it back in the others!'* "

Bert can also allow for the shape of the containers changing. He fills a tall glass L to the same level as beaker A, then adds some more, 'because the glass is smaller: you think it's the same, but its not true.' (Page 18.)

Number

Most children understand the conservation of quantity by about seven years of age according to Piaget's evidence. This means that they can mentally hold on to the fact that a certain amount of liquid remains constant even when transformations of shape and size are made to take place before their eyes. In other words they can discount perception and rely on thought in this area of experience. This notion of conservation is sometimes referred to as a mental structure, a permanent part of our mental equipment which, once grasped, is retained and used. Piaget would also say that children answering like Bert are thinking 'operationally'. (The writers did not find verbal definitions of special terms used by Piaget very helpful (e.g. operational) in the early stages of their reading. It proved better to collect concrete examples of children's responses which illustrated the terms.)

The above experiments with liquid and similar ones which follow using beads (the development of conservation of discontinuous quantities), are not too difficult to follow. It will be found to be helpful to try some of the experiments with children, for until one has experienced surprise at their apparent failure to understand something we should have taken for granted they knew, it is difficult to appreciate what Piaget has really revealed.

The next problem in the understanding of number that Piaget examines is that of 'correspondence'. Underlying the simple activity of counting is the comprehension of one element matched with another. This matching of one set with another is not sufficient to ensure numerical understanding, but it is a necessary part of it. Piaget examines in detail two aspects of correspondence—cardinal and ordinal. In testing children's understanding of cardinal number he devised tests which guided children into making two corresponding sets. For instance, he presented six dolls' size bottles in a row and a set of small glasses. A child was asked to set out just enough glasses to have one to go with each bottle. Once the correct correspondence had been made, the glasses were removed from near the bottles and grouped close together or spaced out. The child was then asked if there were as many glasses as bottles.

Here are some of the children's responses from Chapter III, 'Provoked Correspondence and the Equivalence of Sets.'

STAGE I: NO EXACT CORRESPONDENCE AND NO EQUIVALENCE

"BON (4; 0): 'Look at all these little bottles. What shall we need if we want to drink?—*Some glasses.*— Well, there are a lot here (putting them on the table). Now put out enough glasses for the bottles, just one for each.—(He took the 12 glasses, but put them close together, so that the 6 bottles made a rather longer row).—Where are there more?—*There* (the bottles).—Well then, put one glass for each bottle.—(He made the 12 glasses into a row the same length as that of the 6 bottles).—Are they the same? —*Yes.*—(The bottles were then put further apart.) Is there the same number of glasses and bottles?— *Yes* (but he spread out the glasses a little more.)— (The bottles were then put still further apart.)— *There are only a few here* (the 12 glasses), *and there* (the 6 bottles) *there are a lot.'*

GOL (4; 0): began by pouring the contents of each bottle into a glass. When he came to the 4th bottle he suddenly saw that he could not make 6 bottles correspond to the 12 glasses, and cried: '*There aren't many bottles.*—Then you can take some glasses away.—(He left 7 glasses for 6 bottles, putting the glasses rather closer together.)—Is there the same number of glasses and bottles?—*Yes*—(One glass was then put in front of each bottle, so that one could be seen to have no corresponding bottle.)—*We'll have to have another bottle.*—(He was given one.) Is it right now?—(He so arranged them that the first bottle corresponded to the second glass, and so on up to the 7th bottle, for which there was thus no glass.) *No, here there's a glass missing, and there there's a glass that hasn't a bottle.*—What do we need then?—*One bottle and one glass.*—(He was given them but he put them opposite one another and never made the correct correspondence.)'

CAR (5; 2): 'Arrange them so that each bottle has its glass.—(He had taken all the glasses, so he removed some and left 5. He tried to make these correspond to the 6 bottles by spacing them out so as to make a row the same length.) Is there the same number of bottles and glasses? *Yes.*—Exactly?—*Yes.*— (The 6 bottles were then moved closer together so that the two rows were no longer the same length.) Are they the same?—*No.*—Why?—*There aren't many bottles.*—Are there more glasses or more bottles?—*More glasses* (pushing them a little closer together.)—Is there the same number of glasses and bottles now?—*Yes*—Why did you do that?—*Because that makes them less'.*" (Page 43.)

These children do not understand the problem that is set. They make mistakes because, in their thinking, words like 'more', and 'same' refer to a spatial dimension and not a numerical amount.

STAGE II: ONE-ONE CORRESPONDENCE, BUT WITHOUT
LASTING EQUIVALENCE OF CORRESPONDING SETS

"The following examples are those of children who are perfectly capable of making without hesitation the one-one correspondence between bottles and glasses. But although they are certain that there are as many glasses as bottles when they can see the corresponding elements opposite one another, they cease to believe in the equivalence when the rows are no longer of equal length.

HOC (4; 3): 'Look imagine that these are bottles in a café. You are the waiter, and you have to take some glasses out of the cupboard. Each bottle must have a glass.' He put one glass opposite each bottle and ignored the other glasses. 'Is there the same number?—*Yes*.—(The bottles were then grouped *together*.) Is there the same number of glasses and bottles?—*No*.—Where are there more?—*There are more glasses*.' The bottles were put back, one opposite each glass, and the glasses were then grouped together. 'Is there the same number of glasses and bottles?—*No*—Where are there more?— *More bottles*—Why are there more bottles?—*Just because*'.

MOG (4 ; 4): estimated that he needed 9 glasses for the 6 bottles, then made the one-one correspondence and removed the 3 that were left over, and said spontaneously: '*No. It wasn't the right number.*— And are they the same now?—*Yes*.—(The glasses were put closer together and the bottles spread out a little). Is there the same number of glasses and bottles?—*No.*—Where are there more?—*There are more bottles.'*

GIN (4; 11): 'Take just enough glasses off this tray for the bottles, one for each.—(He took all the glasses). Do you think it's the same number?—*No.*— Take away the extra ones then.—(He made the one-one correspondence merely by looking at them, and left 6 glasses on the tray without counting.) Are they the same—*Yes.*—Well, now put them so that we can see if it's right.—(He placed them correctly opposite the bottles.) *There.*—Is there the same number?— *Yes.*—(The glasses were then grouped together.) Is there the same number of glasses and bottles?—*No.* —Where are there more?—*There are more bottles.* Why?—*Because there are more here* (pointing to the row of 6 bottles).—(The glasses were spread out and the bottles grouped together.) Are they the same?— *No.*—Where are there more?—*Here* (the glasses).' "
(Page 44).

Children at this stage do better than those at Stage I, because they are able to match bottles and glasses one for one. Mog even uses the word 'number' in connection with this matching activity. However, when the visual arrangement of the objects they have so carefully matched is changed, questions using the words 'more' and 'same' are still interpreted as if they refer to the amount of space taken up by the lines of bottles and glasses. Piaget frequently points out phrases in children's responses which indicate that although they can count this does not necessarily ensure understanding of the equivalence of sets. He carried out a separate experiment to test this point systematically: the results confirmed that (Page 63),

'If the child has not yet reached a certain level of understanding which characterizes the beginning of the third stage, counting aloud has no effect on the mechanism of numerical thought.'

STAGE III: ONE TO ONE CORRESPONDENCE AND
LASTING EQUIVALENCE OF CORRESPONDING SETS

"PEL (5; 6): began by putting 5 glasses opposite 6 bottles, then added one glass: '*Are they the same?*—*Yes.*—And now (grouping the glasses together)?—*Yes, it's the same number of glasses.*—Why?—*That hasn't changed anything.*—And if they're like that (grouping the bottles together and spacing out the glasses)?—*Yes, it's the same.*'
LAU (6; 2) made 6 glasses correspond to 6 bottles. The glasses were then grouped together: '*Are they still the same?*—*Yes, it's the same number of glasses. You've only put them close together, but it's still the same number.*—And now, are there more bottles (grouped) or more glasses (spaced out)? *They're still the same. You've only put the bottles close together.*'" (Page 47.)

These children give answers typical of those who understand that once two sets of objects have been made equal in number, no amount of re-arrangement in space will alter that equality. Children who show by their responses that they understand this are said to have achieved the 'operation of one to one correspondence,' this means (compare the results of the liquid experiment) that they rely on their own action and thought and hold to what they know rather than being swayed by what they see.

This experiment is followed up with similar ones, in every case the pairs of objects are of the kind which are usually used together in everyday life so that matching them is made easier for the children because in a sense it is 'provoked' e.g., eggs and egg-cups, flowers and vases, pennies and sweets. The results are interesting to follow especially for teachers of primary school children who have struggled to teach 'sums'. If there is one thing made clear in this chapter it is that the understanding of number does not begin by learning numerals.

The following chapter deals with spontaneous correspondence, where children are asked to match sets of counters or pennies arranged in different patterns on the table, e.g., circles, squares, triangles. Here the children have no external help, i.e., there is no 'provoked' connection between two kinds of material, they have to make two equal sets using the same objects in each. The results are in agreement with the previous ones, showing that situations which involve problems of number in our minds may not be seen in that way by young children. Piaget's account of the steps in understanding which must take place before numerical concepts are formed and made stable makes perhaps difficult reading at first, but the many examples of children's responses are helpful in enabling one to translate his theoretical discussions into terms of what the children have said.

Serial correspondence is a more complicated numerical process than one to one correspondence, for the elements in a set must be selected and arranged in ordinal sequence, the position of each element being determined by its relationship to preceding and succeeding ones. In Chapter V, Piaget examines children's behaviour when they are pre-

sented with problems of seriation. The material used
consists of ten wooden dolls of the same thickness but
varying in height, the tallest being twice as tall as
the smallest. Each doll has a walking stick and a ball
proportional to its size. The children are told that the
dolls are going for a walk, so will they arrange the
dolls and sticks or balls so that each doll can easily
find its own stick or ball. When these two sets have
been made, further questions relating to the position
of the items are asked to see how far the children
understand what they have been asked to do.

Here are some examples of what the children did and
said : —

CONSTRUCTION OF SERIAL CORRESPONDENCE

First Stage

"Gui (4; 6) began by arranging the dolls of his own
accord in the following order: 2, 7, 1, 6, 9, 5, 8, 3, 4,
10. 'Can you put them in order, the biggest first, then
the one that's a little bit smaller, then getting smaller
and smaller till you come to the smallest?—*Yes* (he
arranged them thus: 7, 6, 1, 10, 2, 9, 8, 4, 5.)—Which
ball will this doll have (10)?—*That one (10).*—Yes,
and this one (1)?—*That one (1).*—Yes. And now can
you put the dolls in order so that they can easily
find their balls? Put the smallest here, then the next
biggest, then the next until you get to the biggest
of all.—(He put 1, 3, 2, 4, 5, 6, 10, 9, leaving out 7
and 8 at first and then putting them between 5 and
6).'

We then helped him to make the correct series by
disarranging the whole set and discussing each doll
in turn until he succeeded. 'Now you must give them
their balls. The small dolls must have the small ones

and the bigger dolls the bigger ones and so on. **Which balls** will you give to these two (1 and 10)?—*Those (1 and 10.)*—That's right. Now, go ahead.—(He then arranged the balls, each one opposite a doll, but in the following order: 1, 5, 6, 7, 8, 9, 4, 3, 2, 10).—But these dolls will cry because you've given them balls that are too small!—(he at once removed balls 4, 3, and 2, but in trying to fit them in, disarranged the first balls, which he then rearranged in the order: 1, 3, 4, 2, 5 . . .)—Is there the same number of balls and dolls?—*Yes.*—How many balls?—(counting) *Ten.*—And how many dolls?—he had to count again) *Ten.*'

VAL (5; 6): 'Show me the stick belonging to this doll (D10)*—(he pointed to S10).—And to this one (D1)?—(He pointed to S1.) Good. And what about the other dolls?—. . .—Arrange the dolls.— (7, 9, 6, 5, 2, 3, 1, 10, 8, 4.) Which stick will go with that doll (D8)? *That one* (S6).—and with D4?—(He pointed to S4)—How must we arrange them so as to find the right ones?—. . .—Arrange the dolls: the biggest here, then the one that's a little bit smaller, then the next smallest, until you get to the smallest of all.— (10, 9, 7, 4, 6, then 10, 9, 6, 7, 4, 8, 5, 2, 3, 1.)—Try to put the biggest first; you've got it, look (10), then the one that's a little bit smaller; that one's right too, look (9), then the next smallest is that one (7) right? etc.—(In this way he managed to get 10, 9, 8, 7, 6, 5, but then put 3, 1, 2, 4, then 4, 1, 2, 3, then 4, 2, 3, 1.)—Is that right (2, 3)?—*No* (correcting it.) Now put the stick belonging to each doll.—(He put 9, 10, 8, 7, 4.) Is that right?—(He changed 9 and 10.)—and what about that one (4)?—(He inserted 5.)—. . .— etc.'

*(D = doll, S = stick, B = ball.)

Number

CLAN (5; 8) tried to make the correspondence without previous seriation of either of the rows; D6 for B10 and D1 for B1. 'Where's the biggest doll?—(He put D9 with B10, then D3 with B4, D2 with B2, made the correction B10 with D10 and B9 with D9; D4 with B6; etc.)—How can we be sure that each doll has his right ball?—(He made a few changes but without forming the series.) Suppose you begin with the biggest, then put the next size and so on.—(He then tried to form the series, but experienced the same difficulties as the earlier children.)' ROS (5; 6), after having the same difficulties in forming the series of dolls, put B1 opposite D1, then B3 with D2, B4 with D3, B8 and then B6 with D4, D8 with D5, and B9 with D6. He then took B5 and said: '*I don't know where to put this one.*' He removed B4 and put B5 in its place, opposite D3. Having looked at the whole row, he was not satisfied, removed all the balls and then arranged them thus under the row of dolls 10—1: B10, —, 9, 7, —, 8, 6, 5, 4, 1, balls 2 and 3 being left out and dolls 9 and 6 having no balls." (Page 99.)

It can be seen that children in this first stage have not only difficulty with ordering size in the sets of dolls, sticks or balls, but also in matching two sets i.e., dolls with appropriate sticks or balls. It is worth noting again that even though Gui can count correctly, this did not help him towards the solution of his problem.

Second Stage.
"TIS (5; 6) was looking at the dolls and sticks which were all confused. 'Are the dolls alike?—*Oh no, they get smaller and smaller, and that's the smallest.*—Do you know which stick belongs to which doll? How

19

can we find out?—*We must arrange them smaller,
smaller, smaller.* Of his own accord Tis then began
to arrange the sticks in the following order: 9, 10, 8,
and then said, *No, I've got two the same size.* He
then measured 10 and 8 and put 10 in position, then
compared 9 and 8, put down 9, 8, 7. (He had not
compared 10 and 9 and had corrected his original
mistake by chance.) He then picked up 6, 5, 4,
measured them one against the other, then con-
tinued the series 6, 5, 4, 3, 2, 1. After this he looked
at the dolls and without any suggestion from me put
the 10 and 1 opposite sticks 10 and 1. He then correctly placed doll 9, then 7, 8, (correcting himself
after comparing them) and finally completed the
series 6, 5, 4, 3, 2, the whole series of dolls thus being opposite the sticks . . .

CHOU (7): 'Which doll goes with that ball (the biggest)?—*The very big one.*—Now put the balls with
the dolls they belong to.' He arranged the dolls in
the order 4, 6, 7, 8, 3, 10, 9, 5, 2, 1.—'Is that right?—
No.' Without further suggestion he then produced
1, 2, 3, 5, 6, 7, 9, 10, and after some trial and error
finally added 4 and 8. 'And now?—*I must put the
balls.*—He began by making the correspondence with
the preceding term in the row of dolls, 6 with 5, 7
with 6, 9 with 8 etc., but corrected himself when he
saw the whole set.

CHA (6 ; 6). 'How can we find the ball belonging to
each doll? . . .—Which ball will that one have (10)?
(He pointed to 10.)—And that one (5)?—*That one
(7).*—How can we be quite sure?—*I'll put them like
this* (seriating): 10, 8, 9, then 10, 9, 7, 8, then 8, 7, 5,
6, then 6, 5, 4, 3, 2, 1.' After this he put the balls
opposite the dolls, but making an error of one position in each case so that finally there was one ball
without a doll and one doll without a ball. 'Is there

the same number of balls and dolls?—*There are more dolls*—How many?—(He counted the 10 dolls) —And how many balls?—(Counting) *10*.—So it's the same number?—*Yes* (correcting the correspondence)." (Page 102.)

The responses of these children show that they can make a correct and spontaneous seriation after some trials and corrections. They need to experiment as they go along, but they are obviously aware of what is required of them in the end, unlike the previous children. Piaget places these children at Stage II because of the intuitive way they achieve success. By this he means that they need to match carefully pairs or small groups of elements, only gradually seeing the relationship of these to the completed set. By contrast at Stage III children feel the need immediately to keep the completed set in mind while placing each element in its correct final position.

STAGE III: SUCCESSFUL CORRESPONDENCE AND SERIATION

"SHEN (6; 6), without preliminary seriation, at once made the biggest ball (10) correspond with the biggest doll (10), then B9 with D9, B8 with D8 and so on. In each case he looked for the biggest doll and ball of those that were left, and did not even feel the need to put them in a row, but placed them in pairs on the table. 'Put the dolls in a row.—(He arranged them 10—1).—And now the balls (these had all been mixed).—(He at once formed the series opposite the dolls).'

DERC (6; 10) also proceeded by direct correspondence. 'How can we find at once the ball belonging to each doll?—*I don't know*—Think hard. What must we do?—(He put D10 with B10, D9 with B9, D8 with D8 etc., each time looking for the biggest of the elements that were left and putting them into the series)—Are there as many balls as dolls?—*Yes* (He then changed B7 with B6 and said: *If it was like that it wouldn't be right.*')" (Page 105.)

Finally, children are able to carry out the task with speed and confidence. They do not need to go through the process of trial and error, the lack of hesitation suggests that they know what the series will be like before they actually make it, so they identify the elements quickly and accurately. This is another example of children regulating their behaviour by inner controls rather than being at the mercy of external visual factors. Stage I responses were 'pre-operational', Stage III are 'operational'.

These experiments and others which follow do not provide a set of techniques for teaching number. They are best thought of as estimates used to establish how far a child has come in approaching our ways of thinking. If we wish to bring him nearer to our thinking we must give him further understanding at the point he has reached. Children bring with them to school a fund of experience from which number concepts can be formed. All the time they are actively handling materials and observing changes in shape and arrangement, or comparing and contrasting things they perceive, they are accumulating and organising the basic stuff from which mental operations can be formed when the time for more formal instruction arises. It is obvious that some children will come to school better equipped in this respect than others, but it is certain that all will need further consolidation of active concrete experience, because it is through intensifying daily experience in certain areas that teachers can lead children to organize their thinking numerically and to discover that there are words and symbols to represent these thoughts which can be useful in the solution of certain problems.

This is why in some Infant Schools materials are provided which encourage children to manipulate, order, count, compare, contrast, construct and re-organize. Take for example good provision for home play in a classroom, which would include dressing up clothes of different kinds and sizes and shapes perhaps made by the children (measuring and estimating), cups and saucers (one-to-one matching), sets of bowls, pans, cutlery (ordering sets, counting), dolls of different sizes and their clothes, cooking equipment (weighing, counting, timing.) All these materials and others provide for active handling and thinking on the part of the children, while a teacher can see and seize upon opportunities for talking to the children about what they are doing, using numerical terms to identify the mathematical content of their activities. Similarly with brick building, if a quantity of bricks of different sizes, shapes and weights is provided, then the children will set out to build bridges, castles, houses etc., and a teacher can focus on what is of mathematical interest in the building, e.g., the number of bricks needed in the whole or in different parts, the matching or correspondence of shape or size or weight, the niceties of balance etc. Some of this will lead to counting, ordering, comparing, contrasting etc. The child's purpose is to make a construction, the teacher's aim is to see that in carrying out his purpose the child thinks in terms of number, size, quantity, shape, time, weight etc., because the materials provided suggest this.

It seems worthwhile to labour this point because sometimes children are provided with play materials in school and then are left to use them for entertainment only. While this is valuable experience in itself, if play activities are to be used for fully educational purposes the teacher must be an active participant in them when possible, acting as interpreter and instructor while the activities are in progress. Piaget has shown that young children are dominated by their perceptions, they respond to what attracts their immediate attention whether it is the brightest, longest, smallest, loudest or most prized object in front of them. If we want to help them regulate their behaviour by means other than immediate sensory experience, we must see that they construct mental operations by helping them to organize their thinking in ways which we know will lead to an extension and enrichment of experience.

II

MEASUREMENT

[Extracts from: *'The Child's Conception of Geometry'* by
Jean Piaget, Barbel Inhelder and Alina Szeminska
(Routledge and Kegan Paul), 1960]

LENGTH AND DISTANCE

MEASURING IS AN ACTIVITY common and important
throughout life. Since the growth of understanding
of what is actually being done is slow, time and opportunity must be given for laying the foundations
soundly and indeed for re-laying foundations when
failures in understanding occur at a later date. Much
misunderstanding can be masked by correct answers!
For instance, a six year old child was measuring the
height of an adult who stood against the measuring
device on the wall. The child, standing on a chair
and using, by chance, a 1 foot ruler for the purpose,
marked the level on the wall by laying the ruler across
the adult's head. He gave the height *'Five feet and
some more inches.'* 'How many more?'. The child
then proceeded to count the inches *on the ruler he
had in his hand* (which was still at right angles to the

measuring rod) instead of on the wall and gave, by coincidence, the correct answer, 5 foot 6 inches.

The subject matter of '*The Child's Conception of Geometry*' like that in the '*Child's Conception of Space*', dealt with in the next three chapters) is concerned with the genesis and growth of spatial intuition in general and measurement and metrical geometry in particular. The authors say in the preface, 'To ourselves as psychologists the study of how children come to measure is particularly interesting because the operations involved in measurement are so concrete that they have their roots in perceptual activity (visual estimates of size etc.), and at the same time so complex that they are not fully elaborated until some time between the ages of 8 and 11 (depending on the amount of composition involved in the operation itself). A further point of interest is that questions of measurement are closely bound up with those of conservation, and hence its evolution presents a remarkable parallel to the growth of number'.

In Chapter IV 'Change of Position and the Conservation of Length' the authors are trying to establish the stages by which children come to understand the constancy of length and the meaning of measurement. The idea that an object remains constant in length whatever its position of arrangement in relation to other things is basic to correct measurement.

'If, in the course of movement, objects changed their length in an arbitrary manner, there could be no thought of a stable spatial field to act as a medium and reference system; and hence there would be no stable distance relations between objects.' (Page 90.)

Piaget discovered that children often tend to estimate the length of an object by the interval between its boundaries and, disregarding bends or divergences, think of it in terms of its two extremities only. Indeed it might be said that at first they consider only its furthest extremity, i.e., its distance away from themselves. This is fully dealt with in Chapter III of the same book where we are shown that the estimation of the length of an object by the interval between its boundaries is in itself a definite stage in the process of understanding the concept of distance.

The following is an account of the preliminary investigation into this question.

A straight stick and a long thread of plasticine are put in front of a child with their end points in alignment thus:

The child is asked first to compare other straight lines to see whether he can estimate whether or not they are equal in length. He is then asked to compare the length of the two objects in Figure I. He is asked first, "Are they the same length or is one longer than the other?' If he says they are equal he is asked to run his finger along the two lines and then the question is repeated. If he persists in saying that they are the same, the question is asked in a form which draws attention to the path of movement. 'If there were two ants and they walked along the lines which would they find longer?'. Finally the child is shown what happens when the 'snake' is straightened out. Then it is twisted back to its original shape and the original question is repeated.

STAGE I:

"LIQ (4; 0) can answer correctly about the equality or inequality of straight sticks. He is shown the straight stick alongside the curvilinear shape, 'Are they the same length or is one longer than the other? —*Both the same.*—And if two little men walked along here and here (showing their respective paths)? —*It's just as long both ways.*—Try it with your finger (he runs his fingers simultaneously along the two lines). Is it really the same length?—*Yes.*—And this way (snake straightened)?—*It's longer.*—(Snake twisted again)—*It's the same as the other* (the stick).'

MOT (4; 2) '*This one is shorter* (snake).—Why?— *It's twisted.*—What if two little men walked along these two roads?—*This one would have a longer journey to make* (stick) *because it's quite straight.*— Try it with your finger (he does so)—*That one is longer* (the stick).—(The snake is straightened out:) And this way?—*It's longer* (the snake).—(Original shape)—*Now it's the same as the other* (stick).'

THER (4; 6) '*They're both the same length* (indicating the end-points). What if an ant walked along these two things, would it have further to go one way than the other?—*It would have further to go*

28

on the stick.—Why?—*Because the* (straight) *stick is even longer.*—Run your finger along them (he does so).—Which way did you go further?—*That way* (snake).—Then which is longer? (He hesitates and makes no reply)—(Snake untwisted)— Which one is longer?—*The snake.* (Twisted snake).—And now?— *It's the same as the stick.'*

RUF (4; 6) *'They're the same length.*—Why? (He puts his fingers on the end-points without replying) —And if two little men went for a walk like this?— *This way* (stick) *it's a longer walk, no it's the same.* —Try it with your finger.—*They're both the same.* —(Snake untwisted)—*It's longer* (Re-twisted).—*It's the same.'*

At sub-stage IIA the subject thinks the curvilinear shape is longer after the suggestion of movement (whether this is experienced with the fingers or merely conjured up by the idea of the little men walking along the two paths.) But static inspection of the shape still produces the judgment that they are equal, a judgment to which the subject may revert even after thinking in terms of movement.

FROH (4; 6) *'They're the same length.*—If a little man walked along these two paths, which is further?—(Froh runs his finger along them without prompting) *That one.* (curvilinear).—Which one is bigger? (After some hesitation he points to the curvilinear shape.)—(Snake stretched out) *It's bigger*— (Snake re-twisted). Is one of them longer?—*No, they're both the same length* (indicating the end-points).

PEL (4; 6) 'Is one of them longer than the other?— *That one* (curvilinear) *is smaller.*—And if two little men walk along these paths?—*That* (straight) *one is shorter.'*

BUH (4; 6) '*It's the same length. That one's like that one.*—And what if two little men walked along them, is one path shorter?—*Yes* (the straight path).—Why? —*The other's got turns.*'

LOS (4; 11) '*They're the same length.*—And if two little men walked along these two roads?—*That* (undulating) *road is longer because it's got a lump.*'

SYL (5; 2) allows at first that they are equal, then without prompting says '*This one* (snake) *is bigger when you pull it out. But it's the same size when it doesn't jut forward.*—What if I make a couple of ants walk along these paths?—*It's longer here* (snake).'

AND (5; 3) '*It's the same length.*—And if two little men walked along these sticks? (He runs his fingers along them without prompting—*That one* (snake) *is longer*—(Snake straightened)—*Yes, it's longer* (Snake re-twisted)—*It's the same length* (indicating the end points).'"

STAGE IIB: (HERE PRACTICALLY EQUIVALENT TO STAGE III)

"PIC (6; 6) '*They're the same size.*—Can the shape of this one or this one be changed?—*No.*—If an ant walked along them (the experimenter runs his finger along the two paths), which would be shorter?— *This way* (straight line)—Why?—*It's less far for the ant.*—Then it isn't the same size?—*No, if you put the snake out like this* (straight line) *it would jut out.*'

MOR (4; 10 advanced) '*The zig-zig is longer.*—Why? —*Because it goes zig-zag.*—What can you do to see if it's longer?—*You can go: zig!* (he straightens it out).'

TIN (5; 6) '*The snake is longer.*—Can you show me why?—*Yes* (he straightens it).'

DEL (5; 7) *'If you undo that one it's longer.'*
TIR (6; 0) *'The snake is longer. If once you put it straight it'll be longer.'*
CONZ (6; 6) *'This one is longer because it's all twisted. If you put it straight it will be longer.'*
AG (7; 0) *'That one's longer because it's twisted.'*
NIC (7; 0) *'The snake is longer because to do a thing like that (i.e., make a curvilinear shape) with the other, you'd need a longer bit.'* " (Page 94.)

The results of this test on 100 children were that 84% of those aged 4; 6 years and younger gave 'Incorrect' replies while 10% were correct (6% meaningless). Of those older than 5; 6 years of age 90% gave right answers while only 10% were wrong.

Main experiment.

"*Comparisons of length.* Two straight lines staggered. Stage I and Sub-Stage IIA. Non-conservation of length.
Sticks in alignment

Sticks 'staggered'

The main experiment consisted in showing the subject two straight sticks identical in length and with their extremities facing each other; one of the sticks was then moved forward 1 or 2 cm. (the sticks being approximately 5 cm. long) and the subject was asked to say once again which of the two was longer or whether they were the same length. At all levels, the sticks were judged equal before staggering. After that change of position, subjects at the first stage maintain that the stick which has been moved forward is longer, thinking only in terms of the further extremities and ignoring the nearer extremities. This response lasts into sub-stage IIA. Between levels IIA and IIB we find a series of transitional responses, beginning with perceptual regulations and passing from intuitive regulations to operations, when conservation of length is assured (Stage III).

Examples at each stage are quoted below: Stage I and IIA.

RUF (4; 6) Before staggering: *'They're the same length.*—(One stick is moved). *It's bigger because you pushed it. The stick is longer.'*

MAN (4; 9): *'They're the same.*—(One only is pushed). *That one is smaller.* (the nearer of the two) —(Situation reversed) *That one is bigger.'* (The stick which is moved is always judged bigger; the line of vision may be either from left to right or from right to left.)

NAV (5; 5): *'The same size.*—(Staggered)—*That one* (lying back) *is smaller because it doesn't touch there* (= the extreme point of the further stick).'

KEL (5; 8): Responses identical: *'That one is bigger because you pulled it.*—(Sticks restored to their original alignment.) *They're the same size but they could get bigger* (if pulled out of alignment).'

CHAT (7; 0): *'They're the same.*—(Staggered)—*The one behind is longer.'* (but he points to the end which projects in the other direction.)

These initial responses are of considerable interest because they show how, in comparing these lines, younger children are concerned exclusively with the order of their end-points. Because that criterion is a topological one the lines are liable to expand or contract, without conservation of Euclidean length. It might be argued that the question is misunderstood, and that the words 'long' and 'short' are used in a special sense, differing from our own usage, and denoting the order of end-points instead of the intervals between them. But the problem of interpretation would still remain unsolved. The key fact is that younger children do not take account of both ends simultaneously, which means that they are quite unconcerned with intervals of length between these end-points. Whether or not the question is under stood correctly, they fail to arrive at the conservation of length (............). This is why their judgments of length have no Euclidan significance and are still bound up with primitive topological* intuitions of spatial order.

* * *

What we would suggest is that non-conservation of length is attributable to the absence of an independent reference system to provide a spatial framework for moving objects. Children who fail to establish paired relations between the two extremities of a moving object, will also be unable to link objects to reference elements. They cannot therefore, take into account stationary 'sites' as distinct from moving objects. Without such a stationary medium which is essential to the intercomposition of distances and lengths (cf. ch. III), judgments of the latter

---

*Piaget demonstrates that a young child's understanding of space is at first confined to topological relationships (proximity, separation, order, surrounding, continuity of lines and surfaces) i.e. that he distinguishes such relationships as 'close together', 'apart', 'behind', 'before', 'below', 'above', 'over', 'under', 'inside', 'outside', etc.

can be expressed only in terms of the relative positions of their leading or trailing extremities. These are static relations of order in which one stick is judged to be longer than another because it projects beyond it.

SUB-STAGE IA

FROH (5; 0). Two sticks 7 cm. long with extremities in alignment: *'They're the same size.*—And like this (staggered 1 cm.)?—*I think so* (making certain by replacing one against the other!) *Yes, the same.*—And like this (one stick at 45° to the other and touching it midway)?—*No, that one* (oblique, which projects beyond the other) *is bigger.*—And these two (5 cm. in alignment)?—*The same.*—And like this (staggered 1 cm.)?—*Yes . . .* (verifying by realigning!) *Yes, they're still the same size.*—And like this (perpendicular and touching the base at its midpoint)?—*No, that one is bigger* (the perpendicular). —Why?—(No reply).'

GROS (5; 6) responds initially to a stagger of 1 cm. with the reply, *'That one is bigger because you put it like that.'* However, faced with a variety of angular presentations of the test objects, he judges all of them as equal except for the right angle: *'That one is longer* (the side running parallel with the edge of the table). Then with the strips re-aligned in parallel with a stagger of 1 cm. he finally says, *They're always the same size. To make one bigger you have to add a bit of wood there.'*

PER (6; 0). Staggered: *'That one is longer.*—(The other strip is drawn the same distance in the opposite direction): Are they the same length or not?—*No, they're both longer. That one is longer there* (to the right) *and that one is longer there* (to the left).—

Then are they or aren't they the same length?—
(Hesitating) *Yes*.'

LEP (6; 10) Stagger with sticks parallel. '*That one is longer because it looks as if that one is shorter, but if you look at the other one it seems longer.*—What if you look at both?—*Then they're the same.* (Stagger increased to 3 cm.) *That one is longer and that one is smaller because if you look at a ship a long way off it looks small but if you bring it nearer it's the same size again.* (Stagger reversed). *It's always the same*.'

<h3 style="text-align:center">STAGE III</h3>

SOL (6; 7) Two sticks with a stagger of 1 cm. '*It's always the same length.*—How can you tell?—*There's a little* (empty) *space there* (difference between the leading extremities) *and there's the same little space there* (difference between the trailing extremities).

SCHA (6; 10) Two sticks staggered: '*It's the same as before.*—Why?—*They've got bigger the same both sides* (indicating equal differences between extremities at the front and back).—And like this? (with one stick perpendicular to the other in the shape of a T) —*This one is turned this way and one the other way, but they're both the same length.*'

CAL (7; 7) '*They're still the same, they can't grow.* With various arrangements. *They're always the same length and they'll always stay the same.*'

The experimenter persists in showing possible modifications, until, like Leibnitz, Cal invokes both the principles of sufficient reason and the wisdom of the Almighty, '*Because God doesn't want to make them shorter. He could if He would but He doesn't want to.*'"

It is clear that much more than a session or two of practical work' goes to the building of full understanding of measurement. Much active experience of matching, fitting, using materials of many kinds is needed to establish and refine the ability to make judgments in this field. Much knowledge in fact must be implicit before explicit understanding can be achieved. A child, for instance, who has had experience both of cutting out a skirt for a figure in a material picture in two dimensions and of clothing a doll will have an implicit knowledge of the increased length of a curved surface. Yet, when first attempting the latter feat children almost always underestimate the amount required since they are misled by perceptual misinformation or deformation of the type mentioned in the above examples.

It is not of course suggested that children should do no 'measuring' with standard measures before they have acquired full conservation of length. It may well be that this is one of the activities that will accelerate the process, but one should know the level of understanding the children are bringing to the activity and when and in what connections one should press for accuracy.

In the nursery and infants' schools we find children at first satisfied with very rough approximations in their constructive work and even when they have learnt how to 'measure' with a ruler or tape, they do not as a rule spontaneously use this skill in their creative work. During the junior stage we find a growing awareness of adult standards and a wish to approximate to these in order to achieve efficiency in the object they are making—the book case must stand 'square', the table must be firm, the boat must float. The need for more accurate measurement is clearly demonstrated and is accepted as an objective necessity and not as the demand of a pernicketty teacher! The formal lessons in 'making a joint' are gladly accepted here or in the secondary school in the service of a wish to make a piece of furniture, while if they are given much in advance of this desire they can be of little significance to any child other than the 'born craftsman'.

A lack of real functional understanding of measurement was demonstrated recently when some secondary school children, setting up an exhibition, required five labels of equal size. They were given a strip of cardboard and after much consultation they cut off one piece by guesswork and divided the rest by two and then by two again, and were dismayed to find the result was not satisfactory. It had not occurred to them to use their rulers. The earlier measuring experiences of these children had not been considered in functional terms.

In the junior and secondary school, no less than in the nursery and infant school, children must have the experience which forms the raw material later to be organized into knowledge. In this, as in all other spheres, it is demonstrated that 'thought is internalised action'.

What we want the children to have acquired is the judgment and expertise which will enable them to know the level of accuracy appropriate to the given situations. We should therefore neither waste their time by expecting accurate measurement in their scrap material constructions nor on the other hand expect them to be satisfied with a table meant for use which has uneven legs. The experienced dressmaker who measures and adapts the pattern by eye can do so by virtue of the wealth of formal measurement she has done in the past. She transcends this, as it were, and can take into account vagaries in the shape of her customers in a way which would be impossible for a beginner who must measure in the conventional way.

It may well be that a true understanding of measurement at *every stage* needs to be prepared for by experience which provides *implicit* knowledge as a basis for explicit training. One cannot imagine that a 'working knowledge' by rule of thumb methods could ever lead to the perception of new relationships in, for instance, some scientific enquiry. The technician who can provide an encephalogram for the specialist is not the discoverer of different types of brain rhythms though perceptually he would be quite capable of this. Some deep feeling for the meaning and implication of the units of measurement seems to be present in those who go further than competence in their use.

Again, in mental measurement whether of the Binet type or Piaget type anyone can compute a score but full interpretation seems to need (in addition of course to the relevent psychological knowledge) a knowledge of the nature and history of the measuring instrument itself and the genesis of its elements which has been gradually acquired and experienced in use.

It is possible that one can hasten the process by which one arrives at expertise by setting up the habit of making estimates and judgments which are afterwards checked by measurement, thus establishing a closer link between the measurement and the skill, and incidentally, tending to avoid the 'absurd answer'. It is, too, very possible that a demand for exactness at too early an age can seem arbitrary and meaningless and can therefore arrest the development of realistic ideas of measurement and the place and function of accuracy.

In this, as in other areas, what we are wanting education to do for children is to aid the development of appropriate thinking skills and good judgment.

III

KNOTS

[Extracts from: *'The Child's Conception of Space'* by Jean Piaget and Barbel Inhelder (Routledge and Kegan Paul), 1956]

MANY A HARASSED infants teacher on the first day of them has been heard to exclaim, 'If only their mothers would teach them to tie their shoes before they come!' This simple outlet for our feelings must ever be denied us after reading Piaget's chapter on The Study of Knots and the Relationship of 'Surrounding'. In it he describes step by step the processes by which we learn to tie a simple knot and reveals a complex of cumulative achievements in understanding the kinds of spatial relationship invloved. His records dispose of the idea that tying a knot is a simple piece of habit training coinciding with the appropriate neuromuscular development. This piece of learning is shown as involving not only competent action but a fluid and working knowledge of the three dimensions of space and some imaginative thought.

This analysis will be quoted in some detail as an

Knots

example of Piaget's method of breaking down each unit of learning into its spearate mental elements.

The procedure was as follows : —

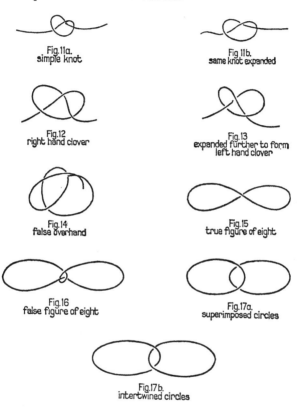

Fig.11a.
simple knot

Fig 11b.
same knot expanded

Fig.12
right hand clover

Fig.13
expanded further to form
left hand clover

Fig.14
false overhand

Fig.15
true figure of eight

Fig.16
false figure of eight

Fig.17a.
superimposed circles

Fig.17b.
intertwined circles

1. A child is shown a simple knot (fig. 11a) and asked to make a similar one. If he cannot, he is asked to form one round a stick and his method of learning studied. If he cannot do this, a knot

41

is formed slowly while he watches and tries to imitate. If this also fails he is shown on two-coloured string.

2. He is shown a loosely tied knot (fig. 11b) and asked if it is the same knot as the first. He is asked what will happen if the ends are pulled.

3. The knot is expanded still further into a 'clover' knot and the same questions are asked. (fig. 12) (The experimenter is trying to establish whether the child understands that there is a perceptual continuity between the three shapes.)

4. The child is shown (fig. 12) left hand clover, and (fig. 13) right hand clover, and is asked if they are identical. He may run his finger or a bead along the string to help him and may attempt to draw the knot.

5. He is asked to compare (fig. 13) right hand clover, and (fig. 14) false overhand.

6. He is asked to compare (fig. 15) and (fig. 16), true and false figures of eight.

7. He is asked what will happen if the opposite ends and the two loops were pulled in different directions. (fig. 17a and 17b).

The answers to these questions fall into three stages: —

1a. Cannot tie the knot because does not grasp the principle of intertwinement.

1b. Can copy knot but cannot distinguish true from false knots or follow with finger.

11a. Can tie a knot but cannot see identity of tight or loose knots or distinguish true from false.

11b. Recognises that the knots are the same knots whether tight or loose, but cannot recognise them when very loose (fig. 12).

111. The correspondence between the knots is perceived and true and false distinguished.

Learning to tie knots. Stage 1 (lasts until 4-5 normally).

SUB-STAGE IA

"COL (3; 10) 'Can you tie a knot? (a piece of string is placed in front of him)—*Yes* (he merely brings the two ends together). No further explanation enables him to improve on this, so a knot is tied while he watches. This is left slack.—'What is that there? Now pass this threaded bead through there—(He passes the bead through the loop)—Now move the bead along the string—' (He moves the threaded bead all the way along the string). Despite this lesson he cannot copy the knot but can only bring the ends of the string together.

Mer (3; 11) does not stop when he has brought the ends of the string together but goes on to remark, *'You can go into the little hole like this'*, and there upon passes one end through the half-loop formed by the curved part of the string. The ends are then pulled and Mer is amazed to see the 'knot' disappear and the string come untied. He is then shown that the string 'must be crossed'. This is demonstrated for him but he cannot repeat it for himself.

GAB (2; 3) seems to be more advanced than the last two children despite his tender years, in as much as he makes a distinct effort to copy the loop and shows by his facial expressions that he is aware of his repeated failures, registering visible satisfaction when he succeeds by pure chance. He begins by passing the string around the experimenter's arm and bringing the ends together, putting the first on top of the second, then carries on to form a true figure of eight. Following this he passes the string around his own arm several times in succession, but without bringing the ends together. Finally he makes a trial on the table by imitating a loop, placing one end on top of the other and pulling. After this setback, he succeeds once by chance but is unable to repeat the operation he has thus discovered fortuitously. Gab is then shown a rather slack knot, but though the experimenter follows the complete outline with his finger, he fails to do the same, skipping from one section to the other at the nodal points without regard for continuity. Neither does he succeed in distinguishing between two entwined circles of string and two loops one on top of the other, despite a few trial attempts. JAC (3; 10) makes real experiments with the string, exhibiting great patience, after he has been shown how to tie a knot. He begins with a loop, simply putting the one end over the other and then pulling it. After this he starts all over again but twists the two ends round one another before pulling etc. Despite a chance success he does not succeed in solving the problem. He is then shown two intertwined circles of string together with two partly superimposed but independent circles. He cannot distinguish between them by eye, even after handling them several times. Neither is he able to follow a partly untied knot in such a manner as to take account of the continuity.

AMB (4; 6), unlike Mer, does not try to pass the end of the string through an apparent loop, but tries to wind the string round several times. The loop thus becomes rather thick but Amb does not insert the end of the string through it. He is shown how to do this but without any resultant success. A rubber pipe, a little less flexible than the string, is put on the table in front of him. 'Look at the snake. He puts his head on his tail (a gesture), then slips it under his tail (another gesture) and that makes a knot (tightened slightly). You do the same thing.' (Amb makes a loop but cannot continue).

Han (5; 3) fares no better than the previous children, despite her age. She forms a loop by putting one part of the string over the other (some way from each end) and then rightly remarks, '*You make a loop and then slip inside it*'. But this is just what she cannot do, for she merely winds the string round a number of times, beginning a fresh loop on each occasion, but never 'slipping inside it'." (Page 108.)

Although the child understands three-dimensional space the transition from one to three dimensions *on the same object* presents a difficuty. A string is one-dimensional but the knot he is asked to make with it is a complex of intertwinements in three dimensions. Moreover, in understanding the three dimensions in other situations some ideas have arisen which it is hard for him to transfer to this particular operation e.g., he has learnt to understand the third dimension by experiences similar to that of finding objects within a box and realising that they cannot be reached unless the box is opened or the side pierced and this is not an obviously comparable situation.

During Stage 1b children begin to learn to tie the knot during actual course of the experiment.

STAGE IB

FRA (2; 11) succeeds in tying a simple knot, several times in succession, despite his tender years. He learns to tie the knot in this way. Seeing his sister

(3; 11) learning how to tie a knot, he starts by winding the ends of the string round each other. Finding that this simply comes unwound, he passes the string around the experimenter's arm, then round the leg of the table, crossing the opposite ends of the string and twisting them together. A simple knot is then tied as a demonstration, though without explaining it verbally. He copies it accurately enough, starting with the crossed loop and passing one end inside the loop. He follows this up by tying several knots successively without any help. After a short interval however, he is unable to repeat these earlier feats.

BAR (3; 6) Whilst we actually watch, he discovers how to tie a knot through his own unaided efforts. For his own amusement he tries to 'tether' an adult by tying a string round his arm. He makes ten attempts to do this, which at first consist of merely winding the string round the arm. He is surprised to find this does not hold but simply pulls undone. Then by a lucky stroke he manages to tie it properly, though without realising how he has done it. He tries to repeat the performance, but without any success until he suddenly happens on the answer: *'The string must be put inside.'* From then on he is able to turn out several knots in succession by crossing two ends of string and passing one through the loop to make the knot, though he is unable to apply this discovery to other situations like tying shoe laces, and so on.

NEL (3; 11) Fra's sister. After being shown an example she brings the two ends of the string together but fails to cross one over the other, simply passing one end through the half-loop thus formed. Seeing that it unwinds itself when pulled, she says, *'You've got to go right round it'*, and follows up with several successful efforts. Nevertheless, Nel is unable to distinguish between an uncrossed loop and a true **knot** at sight.

ZEE (4; 1) After having seen an example, he at first says, *'You've got to make a hole'*, and forms an open loop like Nel's, then passes the end of the string through it. He starts again, this time crossing the ends and produces two real knots, but cannot predict by sight whether his attempts will succeed or not. He next winds the string a number of times around a stick and says: *'It doesn't hold, the string isn't inside.'* After this he succeeds.

TEA (4; 1) Like the children at Sub-stage 1a, he begins by winding the string round the experimenter's arm. But after a demonstration (completed too quickly for him to see just how the knot is tied) he succeeds in slipping the end of the string through the loop.

Moreover, he is successful five times out of seven in distinguishing at sight intertwined circles from superimposed ones. On the other hand, he cannot manage to follow the outline of a partly untied knot with his finger, even when he is asked to do it by imagining an ant crawling through the rubber pipe from end to end . . . (he even tries to extricate himself from his dilemma by asserting that the ant 'dies' when it reaches the cross over because he does not know which way he should make it turn) . . .

STAGE IIA (About 5-7)

ROT (4; 6) ties a knot without any model. 'How did you manage it?—*I pass it through a hole, then after that I make a knot.*' He is shown an overhand knot very loose and all parts clearly visible. *'No, it isn't a knot*—Pull it—*Oh, it is.*—And this (a half loop without a knot)?—*No, it's not a knot because it doesn't pass through the hole.*—And this (loose knot)?—*No, neither is that.*—Run your finger along the string. Let's suppose it's a pipe and an ant starts crawling along it. He can't get out until he reaches the other end. Which way will he go? (on reaching the crossover point he blunders and slips from one section to the other)—And by slipping this bead along the string (it is moved a few centimetres and he has to continue on his own)?—(He fails again)—And this (a taut knot), is it a knot? *Yes, that's on top and that's underneath.'*

VAG (5; 4) is confronted with a taut knot and asked to draw it. To represent the string he draws a straight line and for the knot a circular shape filled in. He then copies the knot correctly (without having seen it made previously)—'And this (loose knot), what is it?—*A loop*—Draw it—(he draws a straight line ending in a curve with a semi-circle rising from the middle)—Can you copy it?—He does so, but maintains that it is different from the first knot without being able to explain how.

DEG (5; 6) reproduces the taut knot correctly, then draws it in the shape of a circle with two straight lines branching off at right angles. 'And this (slack knot)?—*It's a knot also*—Could you copy it?—(He does so successfully)—Did you make them both the same?—*No, this one's different*—Why . . .? Do it again just to see—(he still comes to the conclusion that it is different)—And this (open loops in the form of the clover)?—*It's a knot*—Can you copy it? —(He places the string on the table and folds each end back in the shape of a loop, but without passing them round the central section)—Is that right?— *Not quite*—What is missing?—(He points to the 'wings' at each side of the model)—Try again—(He does not succeed and cannot see the correspondence with the earlier knots). An attempt to draw the overhand knot results in an ellipse with an inscribed angle whose apex touches the curve and whose sides extend beyond it.

Deg fails to distinguish right from left overhands and cannot follow the string in a continuous path. Bor (5; 6) copies the taut knot straight away and draws it in a curious fashion. A circle crossed from one side to another by a straight line, with a half-loop inside the circle resting on one of the points where the straight line cuts the periphery. 'Is your drawing the same?—*The knot isn't tied, I don't know why*—And this (loose knot), is it the same as before?—*No* (he draws an angle with a half-loop resting on one of the sides)—And this (open loops shaped like a clover)?—*It's a knot, but not the same one*—Do it again.' He puts it on his paper and tries to draw it in one stroke but fails. Neither can he copy it with a piece of string. He does not succeed in tracing the course of the knot with his finger.

Gen (5; 7) has before him two intertwined circles of string and two merely superimposed, which look the same but are not linked together. 'Suppose we pull that out (the second)?—*It will come apart*—And the other?—*It won't come apart*'—After he has tied a knot he is shown a loose one. At his first two attempts he is unable to trace it out with his finger (though with the aid of suggestions he succeeds the third time) and draws it as an ordinary half-loop not passed under. He is shown a string forming a loop folded back on itself but with no knot.—'*It makes a single thread because it's not like a knot*—And this (slack knot), if we pull it?—*It makes a knot; no, it won't*—And this (another one, even slacker)?—*No* —And if we pull them?—*No.*'

CHAL (5; 8) copies the taut knot. 'And this one (slack knot)?—*It's a bracelet*—Are they alike?—*No*—Can you copy it?—(Two unsuccessful attempts, then he does it)—Did you make it in the same way as the other one?—*No, another way*—And this one (the clover)?—*Spectacles*—Is it like the others?—*No*—And if we pull it?—*No*.' A bead is threaded on it and Chal is asked to show the route it will take through the knot. He misses the continuities. His drawing shows an ordinary half-loop without any knot.

LYD (5; 11) Like Gen she solves the problem of the two circles intertwined or superimposed, but despite several trials is unable to follow the route of a bead along the string in the form of a slack knot.

LUC (6; 1) says: *'It's a reef knot,'*—speaking of a taut knot and copies it. Then he draws it as a straight line crossing a circle. 'And this one (slack)?—*That's a reef knot as well* (he copies it correctly)—Is it the same as the other?—*No*—Why?—(He points to the spot where the string is crossed)—Do the first one again—(he does it)—Is it like the other one?—*No*—You didn't make it the same way?—*No*—And this one (clover)?—It's an 'Iris' knot (a boy-scout term understood by Luc)—Can you copy it?—(He makes it differently, then succeeds but tightens it like the earlier ones.) It's not the same (as the model of the clover)—Try again—*There it's on the top, there it's underneath; it's difficult to make* (thus he has no suspicion that it is absolutely identical to his previous ones!)' He is unable to trace its course with his finger.

FRA (6; 2) reproduces the taut and slack knots. *'It's not the same as before* (copies it again)—But you made it the same?—*No, I didn't make it the same as before*—And this one (clover)?—*I don't know what it is*—Is it a knot?—*Yes, but not tightened*—

The same as before?—*No.* (He tries to tie it once more, but placing the string on the table, folds the two ends back into half-loops without winding either round the central portion)—Is that right?—*Yes*— Look, (we pull) it all comes apart.' Fra tries again but succeeds no better and has no suspicion that this knot is the same as the earlier ones. He cannot trace its course with his finger." (Page 112.)

Though the children have been able to achieve a three-dimensional intertwinement, in action they cannot achieve it at a representational level because they have not a mental picture of the figure. They cannot re-create in imagination what they can do in actual fact nor can they see the relationship between the tight knot, and the slack knot and the very slack knot nor trace the path with the finger. They look at the three knots as if they were two dimensional figures and cannot escape from the perceptual image.

(Page 118)　　　BETWEEN IIA AND IIB

"KNU (5; 10) draws the taut knot in the form of a circle traversed by a pair of wavy lines. 'Is it like your drawing?—*Yes*—(Shown a looser knot)—Is it the same as the one before?—*No*—Try to copy it— (He makes a few trials then arrives at the answer)— Look, I'm tightning it a little. Is it the same as before?—*No . . . Oh, yes!*—And this (clover)?—*No* —Can you follow the string with your finger?'— (Follows it correctly without a break).

STAGE IIB

JUI (5; 10) copies first the taut knot, then the slack one. 'Is it (the loose knot) the same as the other?— *Not quite, but if I tighten it, I'll get the one before* —And that one (the clover)?—*It's a heart.*' (He tries

51

to copy it but is unsuccessful, forming loops and pulling them apart again). He can follow the knot
accurately enough with one finger, but still fails to
see that it corresponds with the previous ones. He
cannot distinguish the left from the right overhand
knot, nor the false from the true figure of eight.

MOT (6; 3) copies the taut knot. 'And this one (enlarged knot), what is it?—*It's a knot that isn't closed*,
(i.e. not drawn tight) *To close it you have to pull*—
And this (clover)?—*It's a flower*—Is it a knot like the
other one—*No*—Could you copy it?—(He arranges
half loops adjacent to each other, but without en-
twining the ends)—Look (He is helped and succeeds)
—Is it like the one befoe?—*No*. Nevertheless, he
traces it through correctly with one finger.—And this
one (a false knot looking like a true one) could you
make it into a knot by pulling it?—*Yes.*'

RAY (6; 6) copies both the taut and slack knots. 'Are
they alike?—*Not quite, but if I pull it will come
the same*—(clover)?—*It's a circle crossed in a
different way*—Copy it—(succeeds right away)—Did
you make it the same as the others?—*No.*' He follows it through correctly with his finger, but does not
distinguish the false from the true knot and thinks
he will get a knot by pulling the string wound in a
half-loop.

MOR (6; 8) copies the taut knot and looks at the
slack one. He says: *'It's different because it's open,
it's not pulled tight*—but apart from this he thinks,
it's the same.—And this (clover)?—*It's a heart, it's
not like the ones before.*—Copy it—*It's difficult* (he
puts the string on the table, twists it round several
times, producing something very complicated but
homeomorphic with the circle, saying): *I must pull
here, but it shouldn't be crossed*—Look!—(the
model is pulled, producing a tight knot)—Now, give

it a good pull—(his 'knot' comes apart so he starts all over again but is unsuccessful. Then by a stroke of luck he hits on the slack knot)—*Oh look; It's just like the earlier one!*—Is it like this (clover)?—*No, it's not like that.*' He fails to distinguish the left from the right hand clover, and a false knot from a true one.

DAN (6; 9) at once remarks of the enlarged knot: '*It's the same because if I pull it, it will make the same knot as before.*—And this (clover)?—*No, that's not the same as before. Nearly, but not quite the same*—Where is the difference?—. . .—Can you copy it?—(He twists the string about without succeeding and does not understand that it is the same knot)—And this (a false knot like the clover in appearance)?—*It's the same knot as this one* (the clover).' He follows the course of the true and false clovers with his finger, but without comprehending the difference.

STU (7; 0) makes a tight knot and expands it. 'Is it the same?—*Yes, when you pull it*—And this (clover)? *No, not the same; it's got two loops*—follow it with your finger—(He does this correctly)—Copy it—(He makes a false knot, homeomorphic with the circle).'

STAGE III (AGE ABOUT 7; 0)

BER (6; 10) says of the knots (1) and (2): '*One is small and the other is big but not tight*—And if we tighten it?—*It's still the same*—And this (clover)?— *It's a heart*—Is it the same?—*Yes, you must put it like this* (he turns back the ends) *and then you get a knot like this.*' He then shows that the second knot is obtained by slackening the first and that by widening the second the third is reached.—And this left and right hand clovers)?—*They're the same*—Can you follow them with your finger?—(He follows them in a continuous fashion)—Now, are they the same or not?—*Yes, the same; at least they're not quite the same. This is on top of this and this is underneath, and this side it's the opposite*—You didn't notice that?—*I didn't look properly*—Copy them—*There we are*—(at once and accurately done)—And this (true and false clovers)?—*They're different*—Why? —*There everything is underneath* (therefore it is not a knot) *and there it's on top here and underneath there*—If we pull, what will happen?—*There, there will be a knot, and there nothing at all*—Are you sure? (He hesitates and then makes a false knot), *Yes, if you pull here, nothing will be left*—And this (false and true figure of eight)—*There it's a knot and there it isn't.'*

Dev (7; 5) immediately recognised the likeness between (1) and (2), and (3). 'Is this one different from the other? *No* (he makes it). *I put the loops in this way* (outspread wings). Left and right hand clovers: *They're alike*—Look carefully—*Oh, yes, there it's on top and there it's underneath*—And this (true and false knots)?—*There the two branches are both underneath, and there on top and underneath*—And if we pull?—*There it will make a tight loop, a knot, and there these won't be a knot, it's simply twisted round.'* Dev then produces exact drawings of each besides drawings of the three sorts of clover knot.

Now here are three examples of children who distinguish right hand and left hand clover knots at first sight:

Font (6; 0 ahead in his school form) says of knot (2) and the clover (3): *'If I pull it will be like I had before*—And this (true and false figure of eight)? Are they alike?—*No, that's not a knot.*—And this (left and right hand clovers)?—*It's not alike: there it's going up and there it's coming down. There it passes on top and there underneath*—And this (true and false knots)?—*That's not a knot, they both* (the two ends) *go underneath.'*

AND (7; 2). *'That one* (2) *isn't tight. It will be the same and smaller, or like that one* (*1*) *if it's pulled.* —And if the first one is loosened? *Then we'll get that one* (*2*)—And this (clover (3))?—*That's a loop knot as well* (pulls it slightly to demonstrate)—And these (left and right hand clovers), are they similar? —*No there it's on top, and there it's underneath*— And if you pull it?—*There will be two knots.*— Similar?—*No, because they're made the opposite way*—And this (true and false knots)?—*There you won't have anything at all, because both strings are underneath*—And this one (true knot)?—*It's a knot, because one is on top and the other is underneath*—How do you make a knot?—*You have to take a string, cross it over and pass it through the hole* (gesture of intertwining)—And these (true and false figures of eight)?—*There* (true) *it's a knot, and there* (false) *it's nothing at all because it's only crossed, but there* (true), *it's crossed in the hole.'*

GEL (7; 10) Clover knot (3): *'It's the same as the earlier ones but it's not pulled tight yet*—(Shown left and right hand clovers), Are they alike?—*No, different; there it goes on top and there underneath* —How can you make them alike?—(without saying a word, Gel turns one of them upside down, then passes the string on top and beneath)—If they're pulled will the knot be the same?—*No, one will be on top and the other will be underneath*—And these (true and false figures of eight)?—*There it'll come undone; there, you can't undo it, it'll stay put.*

It is therefore clear that the child no longer reasons from simple perceptual intuitions. The shape he perceives is extended in thought by a precise anticipation of the outcome of the action of tightening or slackening the knot, of spreading out the loops or bringing together the separated parts and so on. The child can 'extend in thought' the internalised action so as to be able to predict what will happen when the string is tightened etc.

Provision of two dimensional experience only (e.g., pictures of objects) can never lead to a full understanding of a three dimensional world, particularly if used at a time when the children themselves cannot represent such ideas i.e., make a mental picture of them. Nor can transfer of understanding be assumed from one material to another. As long as a child is dealing with concrete operations the content is of great importance and may temporarily divert attention from the method.

It is of vital importance that children should have both the opportunity for and the stimulus to explore the relationships of objects in space, in order to build up such concepts as the notion of constant order, without which he cannot understand 'between', 'behind', 'in front of' and so on.

We can assume on the evidence that most children of 7 can tie both knots and bows and that, in general, children pass through these stages successfully, but for any child who is failing in this apparently simple activity a further investigation of the exact stage he has reached might enable us to give him better help.

Moreover we must suspect that there are stages in achieving other 'simple' skills which need providing for. For example, plaiting, sewing, knitting, fancy skipping, modelling, and making simple circuits may involve more complex abilities than we have realised. Careful study of these activities and above all analysis of the causes of failure might lead us to a more refined knowledge of what skills to expect of children at different ages, and what mental abilities are being called on in any activity however 'practical' it may look.

IV

PERSPECTIVE

[Extracts from: *'The Child's Conception of Space'* by
Jean Piaget and Barbel Inhelder (Routledge and
Kegan Paul), 1956]

PIAGET SEES COGNITIVE GROWTH as a slow process during which a child, at first completely dependent on action and perception, becomes more and more able to rely on thought as he builds mental structures of time, space, number, causality and logical classes, through which he can organize his experience past, present and future. Piaget calls this a 'de-centring process' because it involves becoming progressively less tied to the 'here and now' and thus able to move freely in thought between past, present and future, and to places distant in space.

One interesting aspect of this increasing range and flexibility of a child's mind is the growth of the ability to put himself into another's place and think from the point of view of that person. Very early in life a child can identify his feelings with those of another, for instance, a two or three year old seeing another child cry will say, 'That boy wants his

Mummy', interpreting what he sees in terms of his own experience. His interpretation may be correct, but on the other hand, it may be mistaken. The busi-

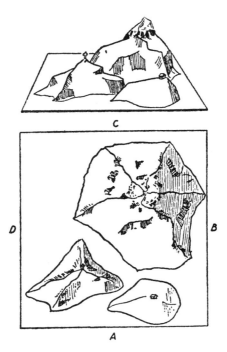

The Three Mountains

ness of understanding the events happening outside ourselves begins early, but it is at first a very limited and subjective affair open to a wide margin of error. However the further we extend our experience and become more aware of the variety of relationships that exist between people and objects and events, the more objective we can become.

Piaget examines this development in children in a number of situations. The one that has been selected for discussion here demonstrates the gradual growth in the appreciation of the relativity of perspectives in space. Piaget maintains that development from a limited and subjective point of view to an extensive objective one, takes place through the progressive organisation and re-organisation that a child does in his thinking as he actively strives to come to terms with reality.

DESCRIPTION OF MATERIAL

"A pasteboard model, one metre square and from twelve to thirty centimetres high, was made to represent three mountains. From his initial position in front of the model (A) the child sees a green mountain occupying the foreground a little to his right. The summit of this mountain is topped by a little house. To his left he sees a brown mountain, higher than the green one and slightly to its rear. This mountain is distinguished not only by its colour but also by having a red cross at the summit. In the background stands the highest of the three mountains, a very grey pyramid whose peak is covered in snow. From position C (opposite position A) a zigzag path can be seen running down the side of the green mountain, while from position B (to the right of the model, relative to position A) a little rivulet is seen to descend the brown mountain. Each mountain is painted in a single colour, except for the snow cap of the grey mountain, and the only reference points are those described.

The children are also shown a collection of ten pictures measuring 20 x 28 cm. These represent the mountains seen from different viewpoints and are painted in the same colours as the model. They are clearly distinguishable and are large enough for particular features such as the cross, the house and the snow-capped peak to be easily visible. The children are also given three pieces of cardboard, shaped and coloured the same as each of the mountains, and these may be arranged to represent the mountains as seen in a given perspective.

Finally the apparatus includes a wooden doll 2 or 3 cm. in height. The head of the doll is a plain wooden ball with no face painted on it so that the child can ignore the doll's line of sight and need only consider its position. This doll is put in a number of different places, and the child's task is to discover what perspective the doll will 'see' in each of the different positions. It is not the child who moves around the group of mountains—except to check his answers—but the doll which is supposed to be doing the travelling. The child has the problem of trying to imagine, and to reconstruct by a process of inference, the changes in perspective that will accompany the doll's movements, or the different positions which the doll must occupy to suit the various perspectives." (Page 210.)

Three variations of this experiment were carried out. Firstly a child is asked to reproduce with the cardboard templates the view obtained by the doll at different positions, round the board. Secondly he is asked which of the ten pictures illustrated what the doll would see, and thirdly he is asked to choose a picture, then place the doll where he would have to sit to get that view. Similar results were obtained from all three variants, only examples from the second will be quoted here. Although Piaget describes development in this area in three stages, he points out in a footnote that children at Stage I did not understand the meaning of the questions they were asked, so examples of their answers are not given. Stages II and III he divides into sub-stages A and B.

SUB-STAGE IIA. THE CHILD CONFINED TO REPRODUCING HIS OWN POINT OF VIEW

"The use of ready-made pictures representing the various possible perspectives enables us to check and clarify the previous results, because with this method the child has merely to choose from existing models instead of having to make them for himself. In the event, children of this level are found either to choose the picture identical with their own point of view, or to choose one that shows everything that can be seen from this position.

Here are some examples of the first type of response : —

"ZAN (6; 6) . . . is now seated again at A and asked to select from among ten pictures, one corresponding to a position near D (grey mountain on the left, brown on the right, green in the centre background). He searches for the right one, eventually choosing pictures I (position A; green right, brown left, grey centre) and VIII (somewhat to the left of A but very similar in appearance). 'Why do you choose these two?—*I saw they were both the same because the grey one is at the back and the other two in front.* —The doll is then placed at B (from left to right; green, brown, grey). Again Zan picks out the picture corresponding to his own position and says, *It's this one because the green one is here* (points to his right) *and so is the little man* (points to the doll, also on the right).'

GIL (7; 4) is seated at A (brown, grey, green) and the doll is placed at B (green, brown, grey). He chooses picture I (= A) and says, *It's because there he is taking* (photographing) *the mountains.*' He then lays aside picture IV (grey left, brown right, green not visible) saying, *This way he can't see the green one; he'll have to turn round* (he is thus assuming that in this picture the man must have his back to the green mountain and does not realise that it may be hidden by the brown one). He then picks up the picture I again, and remarks, *This one will do; here you've got the three mountains, he can see them all.* The doll is then moved to correspond with picture IV. Gil (still at A) says immediately, *From there he can get the grey one, the green one, and the brown, all three of them.* He there upon chooses pictures I (= A; brown, grey, green), VII (= D; grey, brown, green), and IX (grey, green, brown), and discards the rest observing, *He must have all three*—But which of the ones you've chosen would suit him best?—*That one* (I—his own point of view) *It's the best all right because it's got all three mountains.*—And how many are there in the others (VII and IX)?—*Three as well but that one is the best of all because he is in between there* (points to the doll between the grey and the brown).—But from where he is, can he really take the picture?—*Yes, he can, though he can't see much of the green one. That one's* (IX) *probably better; there is a bit of green on it.*'

FER (8; 2) The doll is placed to see the grey mountain to the left, the brown to the right, and the peak of the green centre background. Fer, seated at A,

chooses three pictures each showing three mountains. 'Which of these three pictures is the right
one?—*That* (I = A) *is the right one; he sees the
three mountains just as they are (!).*'
SEL (7; 7) For the same position of the doll, he too
chooses two pictures including I (= his own position). 'Which is the right one?—*That one* (I) *because the little man is opposite* (actually he is near
D!). *It's the nearest one because the mountains are
more like they are from here.*"

Here are two examples of the second type of
response: —

"REN (7; 6) is at A and the doll at B (to the right of
the model). Of each picture in turn he says, '*It's
right; he takes the grey one and the green one,* then
(picture I). *He can take that one as well, he gets the
green one and the brown one; it's got all three, the
brown, the green, and the grey,*' etc. etc. In the end
he expresses a preference for those pictures which
include all three mountains.
TEA (8; 1) also chooses a series of pictures for each
position, one after another while saying, '*He can
take all three.* Finally he is asked which picture is
most correct. Running over the ones he has picked
out (he has already eliminated those showing only
two mountains) he once again says, *This one will do
just as well because it's got all three.*' "

In discussing these results, Piaget draws attention
to the fact that these children all really imagine that
the doll's view of the mountains is the same as their
own. Zan, Gil, Fer and Sel think the mountains appear the same from other edges of the board as from
their own, while Ren and Tea think that every picture
that includes the items they can themselves see will

do to represent the doll's different view points. In other words, children at this level are very much tied to their own immediate perceptions, they cannot manipulate their own movements in thought and say for instance, 'If I walked round the table I should see . . .', nor can they manipulate the objects that they see in thought e.g., 'the green mountain on the right would be on the left if the model were turned round'.

SUB-STAGE IIB. TRANSITIONAL REACTIONS. ATTEMPTS TO DISTINGUISH BETWEEN DIFFERENT VIEWPOINTS

"FUL (6; 10) is at A (left to right: brown, grey, green) and the doll near D (grey, green, brown). Seen from A the most striking feature of the doll's position is that it is close to the grey mountain. Ful therefore, chooses a picture with the grey mountain in the foreground but to the right, with the green to the left and the brown hidden by the green. 'Why that one?—*It will do; the grey one's in front. He's right near the grey one. He sees it first and here it's first as well.* He rejects a picture showing the grey mountain on the left and the brown on the right (as at D) saying, *the brown one is first; that won't do.* ('To be first' must therefore mean 'to be on the right') Ful chooses next a picture showing (from left to right) green, brown, grey, on the grounds that, *it's all right, the grey one is first* (= on the right) and eventually rejects the picture which really suits because, *it won't do, the grey one isn't first; it's the other way round.'* In other words the picture is rejected because the grey one is on the left whereas from Ful's position it is on the right of the doll.

Jos (6; 9) is seated at A (brown, grey, green) and the doll is to his right at B (green, brown, grey). Jos chooses the picture corresponding to D (opposite B;

grey, green behind, brown) and says, *'That's the same thing . . . the little man is behind the green one,* which corresponds to the doll's position as seen from A and not to the actual position of the doll. Jos also accepts the picture corresponding to A (*that's all right too*), but rejects the rest. When asked to decide between the two pictures he has chosen he eventually settles on the first, *because the green one is behind.'*

GIS (7; 7) is at A and the doll in front of him but in the centre of the mountains between the brown and green ones. He then selects the picture corresponding to D (grey, green, brown) and to justify his choice makes a circular movement with his hand all around the mountains, saying *'It's like this one.'* He chose this picture, in fact, because the brown mountain is in the foreground and the doll seems closer to the foot of this one than the other two (when seen from A).

ELI (7; 11) is at A and the doll at B (green, brown, grey) he chooses the picture corresponding to D (grey, green, brown) and says, *'I think that's the right one because he is in front of the brown one.'* However, on the picture the brown mountain is in the foreground, whereas in reality the doll would see it in the background; apart from this he takes no account of the other relationships.

CEL (8; 1) is at A and the doll again at B. Cel looks at the doll for a long time and also at the picture corresponding to his own position A. But he chooses, as did Eli, the picture suitable to D (opposite B), *because the little man is behind the green one and here* (in the picture) *the green one is at the back.* Thus Cel reverses the foreground and the background because he assimilates the doll's viewpoint (B) to what he sees from his own position (at A). After this he also selects the correct picture (corresponding to B) and picks up again the picture fitting his own position. Finally, he says of the latter, *Yes, it's better because you can see the grey one better* (like from the point of view A!)'" (Page 227.)

It can be seen that these children make great efforts to do what is required of them, and they do manage to make a first step away from their own position. They seize on one particularly striking feature that would be seen by the doll, and look for it in the pictures, unaware of all the other relationships between the mountains which must be reconsidered.

SUB-STAGE IIIA. GENUINE BUT INCOMPLETE
RELATIVITY

"STIE (8; 1). When the doll is at D (brown in foreground, green on the right and grey on the left in background) he chooses a picture corresponding to A, *'because not all of the grey one is here.* He also chooses another picture showing the brown on the left, the green on the right, and the grey in the middle. *it's right like this, he can't see all the grey one, it's further back*—Which one is most correct?— *They're both correct because you can't see much of the grey one and you shouldn't.'* Stie is thus taking account only of the fact that at D the grey mountain is in the background and does not concern himself with the left to right relations which he leaves unchanged and hence corresponding with his own position.

LEI (8; 3). When the doll is at B (grey on the right, brown centre background, green left) he hesitates and is unable to decide between the correct picture and the one belonging to the side opposite (D). The former appears right to him, *'because the brown one is in the middle,* but the second appears correct also, *because the brown one is in the middle as well.'* After this he decides on the basis of the before—behind relation but ignores that of the left to right.

DEL (9; 2) is at A and the doll at D (grey on the left, brown right, green hidden by the brown). Del picks out the correct picture and explains, *'Seen from here* (so far as one is able) *the green is behind.* However, he regards as equally correct a picture taken from somewhere between A and D, *Because the green is behind this one as well',* oblivious of the fact that in this picture the brown is to the left of the grey, whereas the other one shows the reverse. With the doll at B, Del first chooses a picture also taken from somewhere between A and D, *'because there he can't see the grey so well',* and finally the correct one because it shows the brown mountain in the background.' " (Page 236.)

In the first phase of Stage III these children begin to discover the importance of left, right, and in front-behind relationships which vary according to the position taken up by the observer.

However, there are so many of these to be taken into account with only three mountains that to begin with they cannot deal with them all, but choose to concentrate on those which are most vivid to them.

At a later time in their development children learn to co-ordinate all the relationships present and become able to predict correctly what the features of the mountains and the relationships between them would be in any position.

Here is a final example of a child just attaining this level:

SUB-STAGE IIIB. COMPLETE RELATIVITY OF
PERSPECTIVES

"MAR (9; 0). The doll is at D with the grey on the left, the brown on the right and the green barely visible. Mar chooses a picture showing a similar relation for the grey and the brown and leaves the green just visible in the background. *'It's because the green is at the back from over there.* He then hesitates before choosing a picture also having the green in the background but on the right of the brown, *Perhaps this one is all right too, because the green is also at the back.* But he decides in favour of the first, *because the green is between the two.* For position B, Mar remaining at A, he chooses first an inaccurate picture, *because he can't see the grey very well,* and then the right one, *because the green and the grey are in front on the left and right and the brown is behind'.*" (Page 240).

It would seem appropriate at this point for the reader to stop and consider how much effort had to be put into grasping the last few pages. How easy was it to visualise the model described by Piaget? How many times was it necessary to stop and re-visualise or look back at the diagram in order to interpret the problem the children were faced with? Those of us who are out of practice in the use of spatial thinking would find this no mean task. But the more effort it required on our part, perhaps the more clearly shall we see just what we are asking children, who are less experienced and skilled than ourselves, to accomplish. It would be interesting to discover if the power to 'see' from another point of view could be improved or advanced by planned experience. This could be provided by using models similar to Piaget's, but it might be better still to ask questions relating to the immediate environment (e.g. the classroom, the school and adjacent buildings) allowing answers to be checked and corrected on the spot.

The above experiments suggest a reconsideration for instance of visual aids in education. Classrooms are sometimes filled with pictures, diagrams and models placed there for the purpose of increasing children's knowledge of the world, but it seems clear that unless the children can interpret these aids into meaningful terms they are more likely to be confused than informed by them. The responses of some of the children quoted suggest that they could not form in their minds a comprehensive all round spatial view of the three dimensional model: one wonders how they would fare in interpreting two dimensional pictures of three-dimensional material and diagrams.

An example of the kind of misunderstanding that can arise in this connection is illustrated in the following incident. A nine year old boy interested in trains, asked his student teacher what a turn-table was. She described it in words as best she could and referred to a diagram in a book (see below).

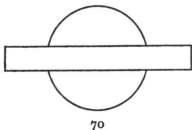

Later in the term on a visit to a station, the boy said he could see a turn-table, and the teacher, surprised at this because they were still in the booking hall, asked him where it was. He pointed to a London Transport symbol. The verbal description and diagram had given rise to an inadequate representation in the boy's mind, it was fortunate that it was possible for him to see later a turn-table in action to put this misconception right.

Another complication for children to deal with in pictorial material is the use of scale. An example of the difficulty this can lead to was given by another student teacher. She built a wormery for her five year olds to watch, and she put an enlarged photograph of a worm at the side, hoping it would encourage more detailed inspection of the real worm. One boy, after looking a long time at the photograph asked, *'What is that?'* The teacher, rather surprised at the question explained, *'But it's not a worm it's too big,* replied the child. Here was one pupil who could voice his doubts. Did the other children merely ignore the neatly mounted and well placed illustration, or did they label it as something else, a snake for instance, and dismiss it as irrelevant to the worm? The student learned from the incident that it is important to know which children can allow for an enlargement or reduction in size of objects when presented in picture form. She has been more aware since of the need for taking into consideration the level of thinking children are likely to bring to illustrative material.

A full appreciation of the subject of geography includes a sound knowledge of spatial relationships. Recent trends in teaching have been to improve understanding of the subject by encouraging children to make studies of their local environment. In this approach a teacher can assume that the children have a working knowledge of the area they live in, for at least they know places and routes that are important to them, e.g., stations, shops, parks etc. By expeditions and discussions the children increase their general information and the teacher heightens their awareness of the relationships between places in the vicinity. The children then represent what they know in model or map form. When they have gone through this process of reducing what they know to symbolic form they are in a better position to interpret meaningfully the maps and diagrams of others, which to be understood must be expanded and connected with their own previous experience.

Piaget shows that it is not until about nine to ten years of age that the majority of children can get an all-round spatial construction clearly represented in their minds. We must remember that this is an average, a few may reach it earlier and some later. Therefore neither primary nor secondary school teachers can afford to ignore the facts Piaget has presented and the anomalies in our assumptions which he has uncovered.

V

CO-ORDINATES

[Extracts from: *'The Child's Conception of Space'* by
Jean Piaget and Barbel Inhelder (Routledge and
Kegan Paul), 1956]

IT HAS LONG SINCE been accepted that drawing can be
used to help in the assessment of children's mental
development. Many teachers will know, for instance,
of the 'Man Drawing Tests' of Burt and Goodenough.
These are simple tests to administer: one asks a child
to draw the best figure of a man that he can, then this
is compared with drawings representing the average
ability of children of different ages.

It is perhaps less often that we as teachers examine children's drawing from the point of view of
their understanding of space as revealed in their attempts to represent it. The pictures with a band of
blue sky at the top and of green grass at the bottom
of the page are familiar sights in infant school classrooms. The gap between sky and grass is puzzling to
adults. 'What's that?' a teacher asks. *'Nothing'*,
replies the child, *'just air'*, or something like that. We
all know the difficulty children have when they first

try to draw a house in three dimensions; two sides which should be at an angle are usually on a straight base line.

A face in profile has its problems too, very often two eyes are represented, and if a person on a bicycle or see-saw is drawn, then usually we see both legs appearing on the same side of the object, the need to show in some way that one leg is behind the other is not realised, and the problem of how to do it proves too difficult. All these anomalies and others can easily be seen in the drawings of young children.

It is quite obvious that children do not *perceive* these things in any unusual way, they have the same sensory stimuli as we have i.e., they never *see* a gap between the sky and the grass, why is it then that they represent their world in this way? Piaget has tried to find an answer to these questions. In the first place he shows that children's spatial ideas rest on 'primitive' topological relationships—things are together or separated, discrete or continuous. For the child the sky and the grass are separated, one up there, the other down there, so that is how he represents them. The person on the see-saw is 'next-to' the see-saw, the more subtle relationship of the legs is not apprehended. The next stage, as Piaget has shown, is when a child can take into account different viewpoints and perspective. In drawings at this stage one finds attempts to make a figure smaller because it is in the distance, and to represent one thing in front of or behind another. But there is still a further development to take place, that is when all objects in a drawing can be co-ordinated, each one related to the others in size, proportion and distance and all placed in relation to the framework of the picture.

It is the development of the use and understanding of horizontal and vertical axes that Piaget examines in the chapter to be discussed.

"SYSTEMS OF REFERENCE AND HORIZONTAL-VERTICAL CO-ORDINATES". (CHAPTER XIII)

"As adults we are so accustomed to using a system of reference and organising our empirical space by means of co-ordinate axes which appear self-evident (like the vertical provided by the plumb-line and the horizontal given by a water level), that it may seem absurd to ask at what age the child acquires these ideas. It will be said that as a result of lying flat on his back the child is aware of the horizontal right from the cradle, and that he discovers the vertical as soon as he attempts to raise himself. The postural system would thus appear to provide a ready-made co-ordinate space, the organs of equilibrium with their only too-well-known semicircular canals solving the entire problem. In which case it would indeed appear odd to want to raise the problem all over again with the 4 to 10 year old child!

Here we touch on one of the worst misconceptions which has plagued the theory of geometrical concepts. From the fact that the child breathes, digests, and possesses a heart that beats we do not conclude that he has any idea of alimentary metabolism or the circulatory system. At the very most he may have noticed that his movements in breathing, or felt his pulse. But such perceptual-motor awareness does not lead to any understanding of the internal phenomena of which these movements are only the outward and visible sign. Similarly, from the fact that he can stand up or lie flat, the child at first derives only a strictly practical awareness of the two postures and nothing more. To superimpose upon this a more general scheme he must at some point go outside the purely postural field and compare his own position with those of surrounding objects, and this is something quite different from practical knowledge . . .

As for concepts proper, everyone has seen the kind of drawings which children produce between the ages of 4 and 8, showing chimneys perpendicular to the slopes of roofs and men at right-angles to hills they are supposed to be climbing. In such drawings we have at one and the same time an awareness of right-angles inside the figure, together with a total disregard of the vertical axis. This suggested that the child has a long way to go in passing from a postural or sensori-motor space to a conceptual one. Nevertheless, the majority of authors cover this distance at a single leap by attributing a full-blown system of co-ordinates to these primitive intuitions.

Hence there is nothing absurd or unreal about the problems we are proposing to examine. On the contrary, it is in terms of the genuinely operational concepts acquired around 7 or 8 years, and not prior to their construction, that the development of reference frames takes place, including those based on the physical notions of horizontal and vertical . . ." (Page 378.)

METHOD OF INVESTIGATION OF THE HORIZONTAL

"For the study of the horizontal the following method was found best. The children are shown two narrow-necked bottles, one with straight, parallel sides and the other with rounded sides. Each is about one quarter filled with coloured water and the children are asked to guess the position the water will assume when the bottle is tilted. Some empty jars are placed before the child, the same shape as the models, on which he is asked to show with his finger the level of the water at various degrees of tilt. In addition, the youngest children are asked to indicate the surface of the water by a gesture so that one can be sure whether or not they imagine it as horizontal or tilted. The experiment is then performed directly in front of them and they are asked to draw what they see. Children over 5 (on the average) are given outline drawings of the jars at various angles and asked to draw the position of the water corresponding to each position of the bottle, before having seen the experiment performed. Naturally, the various inclinations are presented in random order to avoid perseverative errors

(the kind in which a child repeats the same answer without further reflection because of the persistance of an idea or image).

Care is also taken to make the children draw the edge of the table, or the support holding the bottle, in such a way that this horizontal, directly perceived, can assist in judging the position of the liquid. As soon as he has made this drawing the child compares it with the experiment which now takes place. He is then asked to correct it or produce a new drawing and so passes on to other predictions. Care was taken to have the level of the water at the height of the child's eyes, or a little above, so that he can see the edge of the surface clearly." (Page 381.)

METHOD OF INVESTIGATION OF THE VERTICAL

"For studying verticals the following methods were employed. Firstly during the preceding experiment on the jars of water, we floated a small cork on the

surface of the water with a match-stick rising vertically from it. The child is asked to draw the position
of the 'mast' of this 'ship' at different inclinations of
the jar and then correct his drawing after seeing the
experiment. Secondly, we suspended a plumb-line
inside the jars (now empty), the plumb-bob being
shaped to represent a fish. The child has to predict
the line of the string when the jar is tilted at various
angles. This done, the experiment of actually tilting
the jar is performed and the child is asked for further
drawings. Thirdly, the child is shown a mountain of
sand, plasticine etc., and asked to plant posts 'nice
and straight' (upright) on the summit, on the ground
nearby, or on the slopes of the mountain. It is very
important to get him to make clear what he means
by 'straight' and 'sloping' in referring to the posts
(a selection of drawings helps the experiment along).
The child is also asked to draw the mountain, showing the posts either 'nice and straight' (upright) or
sloping. Finally, we sometimes combined the experiment using the plumb-line with that of the mountain, by getting the child to predict the direction of
the string when the bob was suspended from hooks
projecting from posts planted on the sides or on the
summit of the mountain . . ." (Page 381.)

STAGE I: INABILITY TO DISTINGUISH SURFACES OR
PLANES, IN THE CASE OF EITHER FLUIDS OR SOLIDS.
(THIS IS AN EXAMPLE WHERE THE SUGGESTED STAGE
ZERO WOULD BE APPROPRIATE)

"The first stage lasts until about the age of 4 to 5
years. When the children are asked to draw the level
of the water in a bottle or the trees on the side of a
toy mountain their reaction is extremely interesting,
for they are unable to distinguish 'planes' as such.

Consequently, they show the liquid neither as a line, nor as a surface, but as a kind of ball (as soon as they get beyond mere scribbling). They think of the fluid in purely topological terms, merely as something inside the jar, and not according to euclidean concepts like straight lines, planes, inclinations, and dimensions. Here are some examples:

VIL (3; 0). Even with the bottle standing upright Vil can only show the water in the form of scribbles extending beyond the walls of the jar, supposed to indicate the liquid inside the bottle (drawn by the experimenter).

DAN (4; 1) has a straight-sided bottle drawn for him. Asked to draw the contents he shows the water as a blot on the left-hand side near the neck. Yet he can copy lines when these are drawn in, though unable to orient them correctly, even with the bottle upright.

MAN (4; 6) draws the water inside the jar as a kind of little ball situated regardless of the sides or base of the bottle, whatever the angle of tilt. We then drew for him lines representing the horizontal level (or the horizontal and vertical axis) with the bottle in two positions, upright and sideways, asking him to put in the water. He draws his little round blots inside the bottle whether it is upright or lying down.

For the vertical axis, here are some equally amusing examples:

NIL (3; 11). Shown a mountain with a slope of 45°, he draws the trees and men parallel to the base, then two houses stuck to the slope by their side walls, the base of the building including the doors, which are carefully drawn, thus remaining suspended in mid-air.

GEH: (4; 2) draws houses and trees, some lying along the slope, others against the background of the mountain but placed haphazardly so that it is impossible to tell whether he visualises them as located on the slope seen full face or simply stuck to the object.

KUP (4; 11) draws the houses not only sloping with the mountain but turned at all sorts of angles, including one with doors, windows, chimney and column of smoke, all upside down, the base in mid-air and the roof underneath with smoke descending from the chimney at about 20° from the vertical. Yet when Kup is asked what direction one must follow in order to climb the mountain he naturally points out the correct way.

BER (4; 8) draws the trees as did the previous children, more or less parallel with the edge of the mountainside but inside the line as if he were afraid of locating them in empty space. He is asked whether they stand upright or slanting. *'They're all standing upright. I don't know how to make them sloping.'* So he sees them as upright like his own body, though he draws them slanting. On the other hand, the plumb-line (a button hung from a needle) produces the remark, *'It's going to fall to the ground'*, though the line he makes is only vertical when the path of the thread is not influenced by the sides of the mountain but is perceived relative to his own body. In other cases the thread is drawn oblique, not because the button is imagined as rolling down the slope, but because seeing the needle in profile on a ledge overhanging empty space, the child refuses to let the thread fall straight into empty space, but gives it an angle as if the mountain attracted the object instead of letting it fall vertical!" (Page 384.)

Co-ordinates

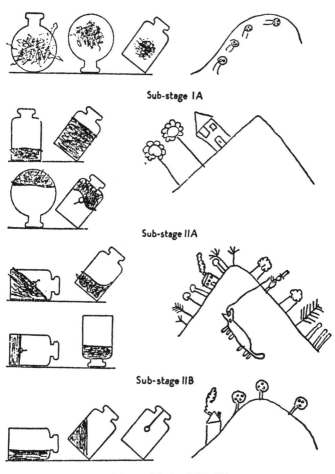

Sub-stage IA

Sub-stage IIA

Sub-stage IIB

Intermediate level IIB–IIIA

These examples enable us to understand the absence of reference to a co-ordinate system, i.e., the

81

orientation of the jars from vertical towards the horizontal and the relationship of this to the water level go unnoticed by the children. The relationship the children present are topological (see page 33), i.e., the water is *in* the jar, so 'in-ness' is represented by a blob or scribble within the walls of the jar, regardless of the water level's relationship to the sides. Similarly trees and houses are 'next to' the mountain so they are carefully placed in proximity but without regard to the correct orientation.

SUB-STAGE IIA. WATER LEVEL SHOWN PARALLEL WITH
THE BASE OF THE JAR AND TREES PERPENDICULAR TO
THE MOUNTAINSIDE

"When the child learns to abstract the surface of the liquid as a plane and locate the trees relative to the mountainside he still fails to grasp the orientation of the water in a tilted vessel or that of the trees to an inclined slope. In the case of the water he thinks of it as moving toward the neck of the bottle, but not by simple displacement. He imagines it as expanding, increasing in volume, and it is because of this increase that it draws nearer the neck as the jar is tipped, while the surface remains parallel to the base.

WIL (5; 3). 'We're going to tip the jar over like this. What will the water do? *It will move.* How will it move; where to? Show it on the glass—(He points to a level 1 cm. higher than the present one, all round the bottle, parallel to the base)—And if we tip it the other way?—(same reaction)'. He is asked to draw the level on jars sketched in outline and tilted at various angles. He produces a water-line parallel to the base in each one. 'Show me the position the

water will move to with your fingers on the glass
again. (He once more shows the water-line parallel
to the base)—Now look and see if that's right. (The
jar is tipped while he actually has his finger in the
position he predicts for the water).—*Yes, it's right.*
Is there any water actually near your finger? *No.*
And if we tip the jar more still, where will the water
go?—(Once more he indicates a level tilted parallel
with the base)—Look—(we perform the experiment
again). Is it right? *No.* And if we tip it even more?—
(Again he shows a level parallel with the base)—
Now watch again (we do the experiment) and draw
what you see—(He draws a line parallel to the base
of the jar!)'.

We now try the round flask to prevent his using
the base as a parallel: 'Draw what the water looks
like (neck vertical)—(He draws a correct horizontal
level)—Now we're going to turn it like this (45°).
Draw what the water will look like—(he draws the
water-line nearly vertical)—(we perform the experiment). Were you right?—(He refuses to admit he
was not)'.

LIA (5; 7) shows the level of the water in the tilted
jar the same way, raising it by 2 or 3 cm., with two
fingers, indicating a line parallel to the base. 'Now
let's see whether that's right (experiment). *No.* (he
spontaneously moves his fingers to make them correspond with the true level). Now draw what you
see (he is given the outline sketches of the jars)—
(He draws a level parallel to the base!) Subsequent
trials show that Lia cannot apply generally what he
sees take place, nor even produce a correct level by
directly copying the tilted apparatus.

HER (5; 3) is slightly ahead of the two previous
children. 'What will the water do when the jar is
tilted? Will it stay where it is or move? *It will stay*

where it is. (He is given two diagrams, one showing the jar upright, the other inclined at 45°. He draws the water horizontal in the first and tipped at 45° in the second). Show with your fingers on the jar where the water will be—(He indicates a line slightly above the present level but parallel to it). Now we'll see whether you're right—*No, here it's higher and there it's gone down. And if we tip it still further? Then it will get higher still here and lower down there.* Can you draw what you're describing on this jar which is tipped over on its side? (Outline drawing of the jar tipped at 90°). *Like this* (he draws a vertical level parallel with the base of the jar)—Now let's check it (experiment) *No.* Well then, draw what you've just seen—(He produces a curious drawing which is a compromise between the vertical position conforming to his own schema and the horizontal position just seen. The water is shown adhering both to the horizontal side and the vertical base of the tilted jar, the water-line being curved). (We now produce the spherical flask). Draw what the water looks like. (Correct drawing). Now we're going to tilt it. Make a drawing to show where the water will go. *It will come up here.* (On a diagram tilted at 45°, He draws the water adhering to one side in the form of a crescent, so that on the average the water is inclined at 45° also)—And if we tilt it the other way?—(Same drawing in reverse).

PAD (5; 8) likewise invariably predicts that the water will remain parallel to the base whatever the angle of the bottle. When this is inverted he shows the water adhering to the base and suspended in mid-air. With the spherical bottle the position of the water is the same but the surface remains flat and turns with the flask. Confronted with the actual experiment Pad reacts in three ways. Sometimes he con-

tinues to make the level parallel to the base, sometimes he divides it into two parts, one parallel to the
base and one parallel to the sides (like Her), and at
other times he draws the water adhering to the base
and the walls of the jar.

These children are ahead of their colleagues in
Stage I for they can indicate the water as a plane
surface, although they remain incapable of seeing
that this surface stays horizontal under all circum-
stances. This may be due to two causes, one physical,
the other geometrical, which we shall endeavour to
examine concurrently. From the physical standpoint,
these children are ignorant of the vital fact that the
water remains always horizontal, though they all
know that when the straight-sided jar is upright the
liquid 'lies flat', presenting a surface parallel to the
base and perpendicular to the sides.

What is so extraordinary is the fact that not one
of these children has ever noticed the successive positions taken up by the water as the bottles are tilted,
or observed that the level remained horizontal;
which, by the way, shows how poorly commonly perceived events are recorded in the absence of a schema
within which they may be organised. Yet there can
be nothing more common for children of all ages
than watching a jug of water tilt until the spout
touches the glass being filled, and nothing would
seem easier than noticing that the liquid remains
horizontal. Notwithstanding this, our subjects all
appear to think that the water-line stays constant,
not in relation to external reference systems, of
course, for this would amount to understanding that
it remains horizontal, but in relation to the bottle
itself. This is equivalent to assuming that the water
tilts with the jar and can occupy any and every position, including the vertical! As the water stays paral-

Co-ordinates

lel to the base, yet nevertheless reaches the neck
when the bottle is tilted, the children simply imagine
the surface of the water rising without changing
direction, as if it expanded in order to leave the
bottle (see Wil and Lia, also Her at the beginning of
the experiment).

The second point to note, is how little these children can be influenced by the outcome of the experiment, guided as they are by the 'false-absolute' of the
permanent level of the water, always envisaged as
parallel to the base of the jar. This fact is important
both from the geometrical and the physical standpoint. For not only have these children failed to note
that a water level is always horizontal in their everyday observations, but in addition and even more
astonishing, they do not manage to note the result
of the experiment when it is performed before their
very eyes and when they have simply to compare
what they see with what they had assumed before-
hand. As a result we find Wil refusing to accept the
facts even though he actually has his fingers against
the glass. Lia appears to admit the evidence of his
senses, nevertheless his drawings continue to reproduce his original errors quite undisturbed.

Now these reactions, as they relate to the child's
understanding of physical space, naturally raise a
fundamental geometrical problem. It is in fact clear
that to take in the facts before him the child must
be able to relate the water level, as he sees it, to some
system of reference. This he could do in two ways.
The simplest would be to relate the surface of the
water to some solid object outside the bottle, such
as the table, or the stand on which it rests. But an
alternative method is available. He has only to watch
the way the surface of the liquid constantly changes
direction relative to the base of the walls of the vessel

being tilted, without concerning himself about objects other than the jar itself. However, the actual results show that the children do not avail themselves of either means of comparison. They do not look to see whether the liquid stays parallel with the table top or whether it changes direction relative to the walls and base of the jar. On the contrary, they constantly assert that the water remains parallel to the base of the jar, and the reason they do so is simply by perseveration from what they observed with the bottle in its original position and failure to observe or structure the subsequent positions properly.

This brings us to the real geometrical problem of the horizontal. If these children cannot even establish the elementary correspondence which would enable them to interpret the facts correctly, is this not merely because the question is beyond their capacity and has as yet no meaning for them? In other words, might not their difficulty in grasping the physical facts in regard to horizontality be due to their inability to develop a geometrical reference system? Now although it is doubtful whether failure to *predict* horizontality at this age is by itself proof of inability to conceive of a co-ordinate system—since it could be due to lack of interest, inattention, and so on—the continuing difficulty in taking in the perceived facts themselves carries an entirely different implication. It undoubtedly indicates an inability to evaluate the perceptual data in terms of the orientation of lines and planes, and thereby suggests a failure of co-ordination as such. What indeed is a system of co-ordinates but a scheme in which the positions and orientations of objects are brought into relation with one another if there is no such bringing into relation, it is because the problem of linking the various objects together in a system where stationary objects serve as reference points for mobile ones, does not even arise for the child. It is because he does not understand the necessity for such a reference system that he is unable to interpret the perceptual or physical data correctly. In concrete terms, although tilting the jars alters the position of the water level, for this displacement to be located in physical space the mobile elements (the liquid surface) must be related to a stationary reference frame (the table, etc). It is the establishment of this relationship which constitutes the geometrical operations that generate a co-ordinate system. And it is for lack of such operations that the child of Substage IIA fails even to take in the physical facts of horizontality. (Page 387.)

This process is even more apparent in the case of the vertical axis. It will be recalled that the child of Stage I did not dare, as it were, to erect trees and posts in the empty space above the mountainside; because he did not know in which direction to draw them, he laid them parallel to the slope. Alongside the discovery of planes and parallels, as just mentioned in the case of the water level, the treatment of trees and posts suggest an analogous discovery, one equally important to the development of frames of reference. Trees and posts are now drawn, if not vertical—any more than the water is drawn horizontal—at any rate nearly perpendicular to the slope, the intuitive idea of the right angle thus emerging to supplement the concepts of the plane and the parallel in rectangular figures.

MAC (4; 6). Puts posts, houses, trees, and men perpendicular to the slope of the sand mountain. In making a doll climb and descend the mountain he keeps him perpendicular all the time. He does the same in drawings of the man climbing the mountain.

He is shown a doll representing a man on the roof
of a house and asked how a stone dropped by him
would fall (when not thrown). Mac draws an oblique
line.

MAR (4; 7) reacts similarly with the doll on the sand
mountain and in drawing trees and posts on a sloping mountainside. Plumb-line: when the needle is
struck into the side facing the child the thread sup-
porting the bob is drawn vertical, but when hung
from the slope seen as concave in profile the thread
is not vertical but follows the curve.

MAR also drew a house on his own initiative. The
chimney is perpendicular to the sloping roof. Finally,
we showed Mar two slopes (shaped like half of a
bell), one with lines perpendicular to the periphery,
the other with lines vertical. Of the former he says,
'they are straight', and of the latter, *'they are slanting'!*

VER (4; 8) makes a very good drawing of a mountain
shaped like a triangle. On its slopes he places two
large flowers with straight stems and a tall house
with a pointed roof. All three objects are exactly perpendicular to the slope.

PIE (5; 1). Both with the toy mountain and in his
drawings he places objects perpendicular to the surface. 'What position are these men in?—*Upright*—
When you're climbing a mountain, do you stand like
this (perpendicular) or like this (we draw a man
vertical)?—*Yes, like that* (perpendicular), *otherwise
you're leaning over*'. Draws the plumb-line the same
as Mar.

Jos (6; 4). Similar constructions and drawings. On a
bell-shaped slope we put a number of objects, some
vertical and some perpendicular. On the slope itself
Jos calls the vertical elements *'slanting'* and the perpendicular ones *'straight'*. But at the summit, those

which are vertical (and thereby perpendicular also) he calls *'straight'* and *'slanting'* those which are really inclined.

SPE (7; 1) draws a triangular mountain and in the space above the slope erects posts, houses and men perpendicular to the mountainside. A man is shown holding a rather elongated crocodile on a leash. This is drawn inside the edge of the mountainside and parallel to the slope. The whole drawing can thus be reduced to perpendiculars and parallels." (Page 391.)

Then follows a section describing Sub-stage IIB. Children at this level are differentiated from the earlier Sub-stage because they realise that when the bottles tilt, the water moves in a particular direction and cannot rise in level towards the neck of the bottle and also stay parallel to the base. They begin to indicate a change in direction of the water level but this may be only a slight curve away from the parallel to the base or an oblique line. (It is helpful to examine the diagrams here to see the changes indicated.)

There is a further interesting fact to note in the mountain and posts experiment which seems worthwhile pin-pointing for the purpose of teaching. When the children have a heap of sand to represent a mountain in front of them, toy posts, houses, and people can be placed correctly on the slope, i.e., perpendicular to the base of the mountain and not the side. But when the children are asked to draw this model on paper they put the posts etc., perpendicular to the slope of the mountain.

Co-ordinates

"JAC (5; 0) places all the objects vertically on the sides of the sand mountain, men climbing and descending, houses, trees and posts. But when he has to draw them he makes them perpendicular to the slope and consequently at angles which vary with it. 'It's the same as on the sand?—*Yes*—Sure?—*Yes*—Try to draw an upright tree, a slanting tree and one that's slanting a lot—(The first is perpendicular, the second tilts downwards and the third upwards)—Which one is upright?—*That one* (the first)'. After this we stick some pins along a slope and ask him to predict the direction of a plumb-line assumed to hang from them. Three times he predicts it as vertical, nevertheless the drawing shows two threads perpendicular to the slope and only one anywhere near vertical (he has a model before his eyes all the time).

MICH (5; 1) stands the objects vertically on the sand mountain without the least hesitation. The experimenter puts one perpendicular. 'Are they fixed the same way?—*No, yours is slanting, mine are straight*—And who is right?—*Me*—Very good—Now draw these posts on the mountainside—(he makes them all perpendicular to the slope, save for one or two nearly vertical by chance)—Show me the ones which are straight—(He points to the perpendiculars)—And the sloping ones?—(He indicates the near verticals)—Which are right?—(The first ones)'. Plumb-line: the same as Jac.

FRAN (5; 6) arranges all the objects vertically on the mountainside, then draws them all perpendicular to it. He is shown two drawings of similar slopes, one with vertical the other with perpendicular poles. 'Are these two drawings alike or not?—*Yes, alike*—Just the same?—*Yes*—Aren't there some that are

slanting?—*No*—Well, now look at these two drawings (a roof with a perpendicular chimney and a roof
with a vertical chimney). The chimneys are the
same?—*Yes*—Which is drawn the best?—*There is
one chimney which is slanting more, that one* (perpendicular)—Add some more chimneys (He draws a
vertical chimney next to the vertical one and a perpendicular chimney next to the perpendicular one)'.
NOR (6; 2) arranges all the objects vertically on the
mountain and draws them all perpendicular to the
slope. 'Did you draw that properly?—*Yes*—What
about having another try? (This time he produces
a medley of true perpendiculars and lines intermediate between perpendicular and vertical).—Now
look. Here is a very steep mountain (outline drawing). Make a drawing of a tree standing on it quite
straight—(He draws it perpendicular)—And now
draw one slanting—(he draws it leaning toward the
foot of the slope at an angle of 45°)'.
LID (6; 3). A plumb-line (string with a plasticine fish)
is suspended from the centre of a wide, flat **cork** in a
straight-sided jar. 'How is the string hanging?—*It
is straight* (vertical)—And if we tilt the jar how
would it hang then?—*It would be slanting* (he draws
it parallel to the sides of the jar).—Look at it with
this ruler (placed vertical in front of the string)—
The ruler is upright—But the string?—*It's upright as well* (New position of tilt, newly drawn
by Lid)—How is the string hanging?—*It's still upright*—But what about your drawing?—*It's slanting*—Is that right or wrong?—*Wrong*—Then put it
right. (Lid finds this very difficult, because he is over-
whelmingly influenced by the parallelism between
the plumb-line and the sides of the jar, and again
draws it at right-angles to the underside of the cork)'.
We now pass to the problem of drawing trees on the

mountainside. Lid makes them all perpendicular to the slope. We draw two for him, one perpendicular, the other vertical. 'Which one is drawn better?— *That one* (perpendicular)'. In the same way he draws a chimney perpendicular to a roof. Finally, we revert to the jar and put a float in the water. He invariably draws the mast perpendicular to the water level in tilted positions (when the water is no longer shown horizontal).

KEL (6; 11). Float: mast perpendicular to the water and parallel to the sides of the jar. Plumb-line in the jar: same reaction as with Lid. Kel has great difficulty in checking his error with the vertical ruler, which he unconsciously tilts to make it parallel to the tilted string in his drawing. He maintains that his drawing shows the string *'upright'*, without distinguishing between vertical and slightly tilted. The plumb-line is then suspended from the cork (a large disc several centimetres across) but outside the jar: 'If I tilt the cork how will the string hang?—*It will be slanting*—Just look (experiment)—*It's straight*— Will it stay straight if I tilt the cork further?—*No* —Well then, you turn the cork so that the string isn't straight any more—(He turns it through 90°). *Oh no, it's still straight*—Now make a drawing of all this (he is given diagrams of corks at various angles and has to add the plumb-line—(He draws them all perpendicular)—Is that right?—*Yes*'. (Page 398.)

Throughout the chapter the authors continually emphasise that growth in understanding is gradual and that between each stage there are many substages or small increases in understanding taking place. Some of these are described and explained as the examples of the main stages are given. These quoted extracts from the original give the impression of sudden and uneven growth which can be very misleading if this is not appreciated. Taking up again Piaget's main theme we come to the Third Stage.

"During Sub-stage IIIA it is possible to see the concepts of vertical and horizontal gradually crystallizing in the actual course of the experiment. Only from the beginning of Sub-stage IIIB about the age of 9 are they applied logically and consistently to all situations right from the start of the interview. Here are some examples of Sub-stage IIIA.

WEI (6; 4—advanced)—predicts the level as oblique for the straight sided jar tilted through 45° 'Watch (experiment)—*Oh no*—And if we tilt it a little more?—*Then the water will still slant a little bit* (experiment). *No it's straight*—And if we tilt it a lot more?—*It will stay straight because it's only the jar that changes*—And if it's tilted towards me? *The water will start slanting towards you* (he indicates this with a ruler which he then raises spontaneously) *No, if we check it with the ruler the water stays straight. It is straight because you are tilting.*—Draw it—(He draws the water slanting at first, then makes it horizontal)—And if we tilt it further still? (He draws the surface very much inclined, then turns the paper round in all directions, looking for a point of reference)—*Gosh! That's not right* (he corrects it to the horizontal and says), *I drew the table first and then the water* (!).'

Spherical flasks. Begins with drawings that are sometimes horizontal and sometimes oblique, then; '*Oh, that isn't right, because it's always straight.*' In the case of the toy fishing rod poised over the surface of a lake he produces a few correct drawings (line vertical and lake horizontal), but also a strange drawing in which the lake is oblique and the fishing rod is beneath the surface of the water; 'Is the lake slant-ing?—*No. When there is a storm, yes. Otherwise it's completely flat*—What about this drawing then?—*It's slanting. But when you put it like this* (he turns it upside down) *it isn't'.* He has thus made the draw-ing upside-down without worrying about the tilt of the paper. Nevertheless he knows how to put every-thing in its place by referring it to the edge of the table!

HEN (6; 11) draws plump-lines for the vertical axis, which are sometimes vertical and sometimes parallel with the sides of the jar. At the beginning he also puts the trees perpendicular to the sides of the moun-tain, then corrects them to the vertical.

In the case of the straight-sided jar tilted at 45° he at first predicts that the water level will be parallel with the base, then oblique (joined to one corner) and finally, almost horizontal. He then applies the horizontal to nearly all positions.

With cardboard models he arranges the spherical ones correctly but the rectangular ones still have oblique water levels in the tilted positions. Then suddenly he says, *'No, it's right when it's flat'*.

WIR (7; 3) begins by drawing the water levels obli-quely on the diagrams of the rectangular jar. 'Hold the ruler against the jar to see if you're right (experi-ment)—*My drawing isn't quite right because it's not straight*—(We continue tilting the bottle). And now? —*I just can't understand it. It ought not to be like this* (horizontal)—Look, I am holding the pencil flat (meanwhile the jar is tilted still further)—*Oh yes! It's quite straight. But that's funny, the jar isn't straight!*—And if we tilt it a lot?—*It will be straight. There's something I don't understand. The water stays still* (horizontal) *and the jar moves!*—And if we tilt it this way?—*It will still be straight.*—And towards you?—*The same*'. Nevertheless, he subsequently has difficulty in representing these various levels by horizontals but he gradually succeeds.

Spherical flask: '*It's straight all the time*'.

BOR (8; 6). Unlike Wir, he proceeds by trial and error rather than by conscious reasoning. Starting with oblique levels running from one corner of the jar, he arrives at the horizontal in the case of the jar lying flat. He is then asked to add boats to his drawings, and makes the masts vertical without bothering about the surface of the water. He is next shown the bottle tilted at other angles and draws the water '*a little bit tilted*', maintaining that this is how he sees it when the experiment is being performed. He finally ends up with a complete and general understanding of the horizontal.

CONU (8; 6) begins with the levels tilted at all sorts of angles, but when he has arranged the cardboard models he hesitates a moment, then puts all the levels in a horizontal series and says, '*It makes one single line*'. After this he corrects his drawings. Asked to check them by holding a ruler against the jar, he says, '*When the bottle is tilted, the ruler will be tilted . . . No, always straight. It's just the same as before*'.

BRAU (8; 6) at first draws oblique levels, then seeing the experiment he realizes that they remain horizontal. 'Could the water ever be tilted?—*Yes, if the jar were tilted further*—Watch (experiment)—*Oh no, it stays straight*—How were you able to find that out? —*I looked at the table*'.

FRO (9; 6) begins in the same way but then exclaims (in the case of a 20-30° tilt) '*No, my drawing is slanting too much, because the water cannot slant; it's always straight because water must always be straight!* (= horizontal)'.

PAU (9; 10) draws an oblique water-line and a boat with mast perpendicular to it. He is shown the experiment. '*I did it all wrong. The water was like that* (gesture parallel with the table) *and the mast was straight* (vertical gesture)'. But immediately following he again predicts an oblique level (experiment): '*No, it's even more wrong*—And if the jar is tilted— even more?—(This time he makes a horizontal drawing, using a ruler which he places parallel to the edge of the table)'. But oddly enough, when he comes to deal with another inclination he reverts to a tilted level, repeating the same error with the spherical flask. However he finally succeeds in producing horizontals in all situations.

CHEU (10; 3) draws an oblique at first. '*I don't know whether the water reaches the corner of the jar* (he joins one corner to the opposite side) *but the float is straight* (vertical)—And if the jar is tilted?—(He draws the water sharply inclined, the float perpendicular to it. On seeing the experiment he at first tries to explain it all away, and reconcile everything)— *It will be slanting all the same. The water will be straight but in the other direction it will be slanting, but it will be straight all the same* (he draws it slightly tilted).—Look at it and use this ruler.—*It's straight*—And if we tilt it further?—*You must keep the ruler straight.*—And in the other direction?— *It will be straight as well.*—How do you know?—*I just think so*'. Lastly, using the movable cardboard cut-outs, he achieves the horizontal for all inclinations, '*because otherwise the water would rise here* (on one side) *and go down there* (the other side)'.

EIS (10; 7) hesitates at first. '*I don't know whether it should be straight or tilted.* He draws the water inclined, and the mast perpendicular to it. He makes a series of drawings all like this, then says, *No. I must*

97

make it straighter.—And if I tilt it the other way?—
It will still be straight.—How do you find the right
answer?—*I look at the edges of the paper or the
table.* Round flask: all drawings correct; *I look at
the table'.*

TRIP (11; 4) hesitates in the same way up till the
moment when, after watching the experiment, he
says, '*It will stay straight all the time. It must always
be straight.* (He corrects his drawings)—How can
you tell if it's right?—*I draw it parallel to the table'.*

Finally, here are two examples for the vertical
axis:

GEO (7; 9) begins by arranging the objects perpendicular to the slope of the sand-hill. 'Now draw them
(again perpendicular to the slope). Draw a few more
posts—(Some vertical, some perpendicular)—Are
your trees straight?—*No, they're slanting.* (he alters
them to make them vertical).—And the houses?—
(Corrects these also) Draw a man climbing up and
coming down (mixture of vertical and perpendicular)
Which is drawn best? (Points to the vertical)—Can
you add some trees? (He draws them all vertical)'.

CARL (8; 2) draws a mountain with rows of trees, men
etc. He starts off with a mixture of perpendiculars
and near verticals, but gradually corrects himself until he draws only vertical objects' . . .

. . . We must now enquire how the vertical and
horizontal come to be discovered. This may seem a
difficult question to answer, but we shall find that the
children whose reactions we have just summarized
will enable us to deal with it quite simply. In one
sense, the discovery can indeed be said to derive from
the fact that the water remains level and the plumb-
line falls true. But these facts can only be noted and
generalized deductively through being incorporated
in a network of co-ordinating schemata whose or-

ganization will result in a system of reference.

The most striking thing is, of course, the way in which the children infer the physical law from what they see, particularly as regards the horizontal in the case of the water-level. Thus, Wei finds his predictions constantly contradicted by the experiment and is eventually compelled to admit that the water 'is always straight'. Wir goes still further in formulating the law empirically, 'there's something I don't understand; the water stays still and the jar moves'. It is evident that without the experiments the child would not succeed in discovering that the liquid remains horizontal, for this is given empirically, and not deduced a priori. But why is this experiment not effective until Stage III? Why does it take so long to produce, first a simple observation (not possible at Stage I) and then a general inference (not possible at Stage II)? In other words, why are these children the first to conclude that the water will 'always' be horizontal, on the basis of noting a few experimental facts?

It is at this point that one realizes the indispensable rôle of a frame of reference. In order to recognize that the water is permanently horizontal and the masts or plumb-lines permanently vertical, regardless of the tilt of the jar, it is necessary—even without drawing, but only by holding a ruler in line with the water or the plumb-line—to establish a relationship between the water or the thread, the ruler, and a set of objects external to the jar. For otherwise there is nothing to show whether the orientation of the water has or has not altered through being involved in the movement of the container (just as a relative movement cannot be understood without a system of reference). Now it is remarkable to observe that the children are, as a rule, more or less consciously aware of the need for an external anchorage. Thus Wei (the empirical nature of whose discoveries we have just commented upon), after having produced the correct drawings, says, 'I drew the table first, and then the water'. Brau states that he 'looks at the table' in drawing the water-line; Pau clearly aligns his ruler with the edge of the paper or the table though he does not say so; Eis admits openly, 'I look at the edge of the table'; and Trip says, 'I drew (it) parallel to the table'. True enough, one could very well ask them what they compare the level of the table with, and this would, in the last resort, refer them back to the level of the water. But it is quite evident, so far as the second aspect of the child's reactions is concerned, that it is no longer the physical problem which is important, but rather the geometrical problem of bringing into relation different directions in terms of angles, parellelism, order and distance. In short, by means of a comprehensive system, and this is precisely the beginning of a system of co-ordinate axes.

* * *

In Sub-stage IIIB, the children know that the water stays horizontal, the masts and the plumb-lines upright, and apply these concepts with the jar at all angles of tilt.

SAN (6; 6) 'What will the water do if we tilt this bottle?—*It will stay like this* (marks a horizontal line on the glass with his finger). Draw it (Drawn horizontal)—*It stays flat like this*—And if we tilt it still more?—*It will always stay flat*'.

STEI (6; 7) draws the levels horizontal and the masts vertical right away. 'Why do you draw the water like that?—*Because it always stays straight!* Drawings and movable cut-outs to be placed in rank order are all arranged correctly.

LEY (7; 0) hesitates for a moment when drawing the water level oblique then exclaims, *'No, no, the water never rises'*. The movable cut-outs are at once arranged correctly. The plumb-line is drawn vertical for all positions of the jar.

HAN (7; 3) also hesitates for a moment, then says, *'It's the bottle that's tilted. The water stays straight, it doesn't stick to the bottle, it remains straight when you tilt it. If you turn this cupboard upside down the animals inside would fall down, but the water in the bottle always stays straight.* He then draws a few horizontal levels and in order to be sure that 'it's straight' he measures the distance between the surface of the water and the side of the bottle (on the drawing of the bottle lying flat). With the next drawing he notices that this check is not adequate and employs the edge of the table as a guide.

WAG (8; 5). *'The water must always be straight; it stays like this'*. Plumb-line also correct.

PAS (9; 6). *'It stays horizontal.*—And the plumb-line? —*Vertical*—How do you know that's right?—*I can tell at a glance.*—Can you check it with this ruler?' (He moves the ruler from the table to the level of the water to indicate the parallelism, then draws the table on his sheet of paper and measures the distance between the water and the table at both ends of the water-line he has drawn). And what about the plumb-line?—(He checks the vertical by eye, looking in turn at each right-angle between the line and the table)'.

COI (10; 7). *'It is horizontal*—What do you do to make sure of drawing it right?—*I look at the table'*.

CUE (11; 1). *'The level is straight because the water always stays horizontal*—How can you tell for certain?—*You can measure it to see whether it's the same distance from the base on the right or the left* —And what about the plumb-line?—(He turns the paper round through 90°). *It makes a right-angle (each side)'.*

TIS (11; 6). *'The level is always horizontal.* I draw it like the table—How can you see it is horizontal?— *I say the base is horizontal and I draw the water in relation to the base'.* He makes an excellent drawing in full perspective on a level sheet of paper, then transfers it to a sheet placed in the skew, showing the horizontal parallel with the lower edge of the paper and the verticals perpendicular to it.

Here are a few examples dealing only with verticals.

LAI (6; 10) draws a mountain with objects placed vertical on the slopes. On an outline drawing of a mountain the plumb-line is always placed vertical, independent of slopes and ledges. The fishing rod with a weighted line is drawn vertical for all positions.

DAN (7; 6), Clai (8; 6), and Fred (9; 3). Same reactions. Fred is shown a house drawn perpendicular to a slope; *'Gosh! the bricks will all come tumbling down. No-one ever saw a house like that!'."* (Page 406.)

Piaget concludes the chapter with the following paragraph: —

To conclude this discussion, we may make these final observations. Topological relations are relations which remain purely internal to each object or pattern. As against this, euclidean relations, completed by the construction of reference frames, are essentially relations established between numbers of objects or patterns (though also influencing their internal structure) and serve to locate them within an organized whole forming an all-embracing system. This is why horizontal-vertical axes are constructed at the same time as perspectives are co-ordinated, for these latter also constitute overall systems linking together objects or patterns. But projective space is in essence a co-ordination both of viewpoints—actual or virtual—and of the figures considered in relation to these viewpoints. Co-ordinates, on the other hand, which express the structure of euclidean space, link together objects considered as such, in their objective positions and displacements, and at relative distances. The age of 9 or thereabouts, which lies midway through the period in which concrete operations first take shape, thus marks a decisive turning point in the development of spatial concepts; that of the completion of the framework appropriate to comprehensive euclidean and projective systems". (Page 418.)

It is demonstrated that most average children, though they live in a world full of examples of vertical and horizontal planes, cannot represent these until quite late in their development. Children have very real experience of the upright for after all they labour in infancy to attain it and benefit greatly from the achievement, but this experience alone and all the others they have with objects around them are not sufficient to enable them to abstract particular relationships of lines, planes, and angles without considerably re-organizing and correcting their understanding as they go along. Here is where a teacher's help is valuable, not merely to tell children of the existence of laws and relationships, but to see that, when they are present in the material a child is using, his attention is drawn to them. One can see that the time and effort needed to direct the attention of very young children to the nature of the level of water would probably be mis-spent. Similarly to try to correct drawings at this stage would do no more than perhaps stop the child drawing at all. Somewhere between 7 and 9 years of age nearly all children are capable of coming to this spatial understanding, and therefore situations in which discussions of this kind of topic can arise need to be provided.

It has been shown that children can represent spatial relationships in three dimensional model form before doing the same on two dimensional paper. The full use of real materials must surely help to lead to good representation, therefore it would seem essential for teachers of young children to provide for a great deal of experience in three dimensional form, e.g., scrap material modelling, brick building, and, sewing, water, clay, woodwork etc., so that choice of media is available for expressing ideas in as accurate a way as possible. One of the outstanding contributions of modern physical education is the increased awareness it fosters of spatial dimensions in relation both to one's own body and its environment.

If children cannot represent objects in correct proportion and orientation, what information can they get from pictures? There are facts they can interpret satisfactorily, but it would seem that any point of size, proportion or distance that we wished to illustrate by use of pictures or diagrams could be lost or mis-interpreted by some children (examples from previous chapter). This is not to say that we should never use such material, but we need to be aware of what the children are making of it, being prepared for differences between their ideas and ours. When it is necessary for this gap to be bridged, the skill of teaching comes in, because helping children to see something from our point of view may mean forming many intermediary steps in understanding.

It can happen too often that children are asked to draw a picture to enable them to recall the content of a lesson, with the intention that this shall reinforce the verbal material given to help them remember what has been taught. It seems likely that asking young children to interpret words into visual images and then into pictures may sometimes be so difficult for them that they distort the original content to the point of confusion rather than increasing the clearness of their remembering.

From all children we expect spontaneous drawing about subjects they are interested in, but the subject matter of their interests changes from the five year old, who only wants to draw himself and his family, to the junior school child who wants to record observations he has made in studying some natural phenomena. The five year old's impetus is largely emotional, and we accept the weirdness of his bodiless figures, with their straggly arms and legs, realising that they are important representations to him. But the older child, who has been encouraged by adults to use his senses more keenly in noticing changes taking place in the world around him, needs particular help to develop the ability to record accurately what he notices. The above experiments show how much help is needed for it is difficult for children to draw what they see correctly, unless it already coincides with what they know (as Piaget has pointed out 'How poorly commonly perceived events are recorded in the absence of a schema within which they may be organized'). It is easier to assume that children's drawing ability is poor when they misrepresent rather than to realize that it is their thinking that is undeveloped in that area. The phrase 'hand-eye co-ordination' bedevils education, it is so quick to say, that the inexperienced pick it up and act on it as if a direct link could be trained between hand and eye without involving mental processes. Professor Piaget dispels this notion once and for all: this, while making a teacher's task more complex, should surely lead to greater success in the main task of aiding children's growth and understanding.

This chapter deals entirely with primary school children, but on them rests the future learning of secondary school pupils. How many children are there, one wonders, who are never helped to make conscious their apprehension of 'different points of view' or a comprehensive co-ordinate system of reference, so that they move from primary to secondary stage in their education with inadequate thinking structures on which to build the more elaborate subject matter they will have presented to them.

VI

'FLOATING AND SINKING'

[Extracts from: *'The growth of Logical Thinking'* by
Jean Piaget and Barbel Inhelder (Routledge and
Kegan Paul), 1958]

YOUNG CHILDREN have a natural interest in water.
Babies enjoy the rituals of the bath, and when they
are old enough to walk they like paddling in puddles
or trying to join in washing up or scrubbing floors,
and many are the harassed parents who have found
the bathroom awash because a child has put the plug
in the basin and turned on both taps. Most people, if
they went into the reception class of an infants
school, seeing among all other provisions a water
trolley with five year olds playing round it, pouring
water into tubes, funnels and other containers, would
smile with pleasure at the children's enjoyment. But
the same people going into a class of six or seven
year olds, or even a junior class, would feel surprised
if not perturbed, at the sight of children playing in
this way. Yet to the keen observer or the person who
will spend time watching the children's play without
judging it to be 'too young', or 'too old' will be struck

by the complete absorption of children as they experiment with these materials. Even young children can concentrate for long periods as they vary the ways of handling water, combining and reversing actions, finding further use for containers etc.

Teachers who have recognized that the intensity of absorbtion in the material itself has value for children's development have been prepared to have this provision available in classrooms throughout the infants' school and sometimes even in junior classes, but the specific intellectual purposes underlying the experimental play have not always been clearly known (i.e., that these experiences lead on to the understanding of such concepts as weight, volume, capacity etc.).

The chapter in 'The Growth of Logical Thinking' on the Law of Floating Bodies seems to make clear the need for constant experimentation throughout the primary school in order that eventually children will have the bases for understanding and formulating scientific laws, such as those governing floating and sinking.

The apparatus used in this experiment is a bucket of water and a number of different kinds of objects made of metal, wood, cork, paper etc. Also included in the assortment is a cube of wood, a cube of iron and a plastic cube, all having the same volume (see use of these at Stage III). Children between four and fourteen years are interviewed individually. Each subject is given the above material and is asked to classify the objects into two groups, those that will sink and those that will float. Then having done that the subject is allowed to experiment in the water to find out what happens when his predictions are put to the test. He is encouraged to verbalize his observations and to try to formulate a possible law to account for what is happening.

Before the law can be formulated two relationships must be understood: density, i.e., the relationship of weight to volume, and specific gravity, i.e., the relation between the weight of an object and the weight of the water it displaces. From the outset we can see that young children could not possibly be expected to deal with such complicated relationships, but it is revealing to see how they explain in their own ways the common sight of something sinking or floating.

Stage I. The children at this stage (likely to include most children in our infants' schools) have no real knowledge to act on when sorting objects into those that will float and those that will sink. They respond to each question with an answer that explains only one particular instance, and the next question is for the child a completely different situation which bears no relation to the previous one, therefore he is as likely to contradict himself as not, and be quite satisfied with the result. Towards the end of this stage some children begin to relate perhaps two objects and one can see how the clever questioning of the experimenter begins to focus a child's thinking so that he pays attention to those elements that will lead him to understanding.

SUB-STAGE IA

"IEA (4 years) says for example, of a piece of wood that, *'It stays on top. The other day I threw one in the water and it stayed on top.* But a moment later:

Wood? It will swim anywhere—And this one (a smaller piece)—*The little wood will sink*—But you told me that the wood would swim.—*No. I didn't say so.* On the first presentation of a wire, he says, *The wire goes to the bottom* (he has not done the experiment)—And this weight?—(metal)—*It will swim*—The wood?—*It will swim anywhere*—The wire?—(third presentation)—*It will swim.* Finally, for two metal needles of identical appearance he says the opposite: —This one?—*It will float*—And that one?—*It will sink.* We must add that although Iea generalizes little, his explanations can be reduced to the format: —The pebble?—*It will sink*—Why?— *Because it stays on the bottom'.*

Mic (5 years), predicts that a plank will sink. The experiment which follows does not induce him to change his mind: (He leans on the plank with all his strength to keep it under the water). *'You want to stay down silly!*—Will it always stay on the water?—*Don't know*—Can it stay at the bottom another time?—*Yes'.*

SUB-STAGE IB

At Sub-stage IB the child tries to classify the objects in a stable way into floating and non-floating, but he does not achieve a coherent classification for the following three reasons (the first of these is logically legitimate, but the other two relate to pre-operational thinking: (1) Since the law is not discovered (although he begins to look for it) the subject is satisfied with multiple explanations leading to a series of sub-classes difficult to arrange hierarchically; (2) In the face of the experimental situation, he finds new explanations and thus adds new divisions to his classification but does not reorganize

Floating and Sinking

the whole; (3) There are contradictions between some of these classes. (Page 22.)

Tosc (5; 6). After having said in reference to the plank, *'It goes to the bottom.*—Why?—*Because it is heavy,* adds a little while later, *Because it is big.* Then he sees that the plank floats and explains the fact as follows; *It's too big and then there's too much water* (to touch the bottom). A moment later he tries to hold it at the bottom with another plank and a wooden ball; the two come back up *because this plank is bigger and it came back up.*—And why does the ball come up?—*Because it's smaller*—And this cover?—*It will come back up.*—Why?—*Because it is smaller than this piece of wood, than the plank* —Try—*It stayed down because I pushed too high up!.*

Bez (5; 9) explains the floating by the weight (inversely to Tosc): 'Why do these things (previously classified) go to the bottom?—*They are little things.* —Why do the little ones go to the bottom?—*Because they aren't heavy, they don't swim on top because it's too light.*—And these?—(class of floating objects)—*Because they are heavy they swim on the water.* We go on to the experiment: the key sinks, —*Because it's too heavy to stay on top*—Whereas the cover sinks—*Because it's light.* Comparing two keys: the larger does not stay above water, *Because it's light.*—And the little one?—*It will go to the bottom too*—Why?—*Because it's too light'.*

Gio (6; 0). 'These things (previously classified) go to the bottom?—*Yes, that one* (the wooden ball)— Why?—*Because it's heavy.*—And these? (The class of floating objects)—*That one swims because it's light.* We do the experiment with the cover. It floats, *because it's light*—And if you push it? (It sinks)—*It's because it's light and light things never*

111

stay on the top—And that plank?—*It will stay on top?*—Why? *Because it's heavy*—Why?—*Because it's big*—And if you lean on it? (he does)—*It comes back up because it's light*—And this? (large needle) *It goes to the bottom because it's big*—And that? (metal plate) If you push? *It will stay at the bottom* —Why? *Because it's light.'*

ELI (6; 10). 'That? (candle)—*It goes to the bottom* —Why?—*Because it's round.* And that? (*ball*)—*It stays on top*—Why?—*Because it's round too.* Thus the contradiction does not only relate to weight. And that needle? (placed on the water)—*It floats because it's light.*—And if you push?—*It will go under*— Why?—*Because it will be heavy'.* Here contradiction goes with nonconservation. (Page 26.)

SUB-STAGE IIA

The behaviour of the 7-9 year old subjects is marked by an effort to remove the main contradiction—which until this they have not noticed; that certain large objects can float and certain small ones sink without this fact excluding the idea that the light ones float and not the heavy. The contradiction tends at this point to be surmounted by a revision of the concept of weight, now seen in relation to that of volume i.e., the child begins to renounce the notion of absolute weight in order to look toward density and, above all, toward specific gravity. BAR (7; 11) first classifies the bodies into three categories: those which float because they are light (wood, matches, paper and the aluminium cover): those which sink because they are heavy (large and small keys, pebbles of all sizes, ring clamps, needles and nails, metal cylinder, eraser): and those which remain suspended at a mid-way point (fish). 'The needle?—*It goes down because it's iron*—And the key?—*It sinks too*—And the small things? (nails, ring clamps)—*They are iron too.*—And this little pebble?—*It's heavy because it's stone*—And the little nail?—*It's just a little heavy*—And the cover, why does it stay up?—*It has edges and sinks if it's filled with water*—Why?—*Because it's iron'.*

Duf (7; 6). 'That ball?—*It stays on top. It's wood; it's light*—And this key?—*Goes down. It's iron; it's heavy*—Which is heavier, the key or the ball?—*The ball*—Why does the key sink?—*Because it's heavy*—And then the nail?—*It's light but it sinks anyway. It's iron, and iron always goes under'.* (Page 28.)

SUB-STAGE IIB

Bar (9 years). (Class 1) Floating objects: ball, pieces of wood, cork and an aluminium plate. (Class 2) Sinking objects: keys, metal weights, needles, stones, large block of wood, and a piece of wax. (Class 3) Objects which may either float or sink: covers. Later Bar sees a needle at the bottom of the water and says, '*Ah. They are too heavy for the water, so the water can't carry them*—And the tokens?—*I don't know; they are more likely to go under*—Why do these things float?—(Class 1)—*Because they are quite light.*—And the covers?—*They can go to the bottom because the water can come over the top.*—And why do these things sink? (Class 2)—*Because they are heavy.*—The big block of wood?—*It will go under* Why?—*There is too much water for it to stay up.*—And the needles?—*They are lighter*—So?—*If the wood were the same size as the needle it would be lighter.*—Put the candle in the water. Why does it stay up?—*I don't know.*—And the cover?—*It's iron, that's not too heavy and there is enough water to carry it.*—And now?—(it sinks)—*That's because the water got inside.* And put the wooden block in—

Ah, because it's wood that is wide enough not to sink.—If it were a cube? *I think that it would go under.* And if you push it under?—*I think that it would come back up.* And if you push this plate? (aluminium). *It would stay at the bottom*—Why?— Because *the water weighs on the plate.* Which is heavier, the plate or the wood? *The piece of wood.* —Then why does the plate stay on the bottom?— *Because it's a little lighter than the wood, when there is water on top there is less resistance, and it can stay down. The wood has resistance and it comes back up.*—And this little piece of wood?—*No, it will come back up because it is even lighter than the plate.*—And if we begin again with this large piece of wood in the smallest bucket, will the same thing happen? *No it will come back up because the water isn't strong enough: there is not enough weight from the water'.*

BRU (9 years). '*The water can't carry the pebbles. The wood can be carried.* And if it is pushed under? —*It will come back up because the water isn't strong enough: there isn't enough weight of water.* (This time the weight operates to maintain it at the bottom and no longer to carry it!) And a moment later, *The wood comes up when you let go because it springs up'.* (Page 33).

* * *

On the whole, Sub-stage IIB shows significant progress in the direction of freedom from contradictions and in the search for a single explanation based on the child beginning to see a relationship between weight and volume as implied by the notion of a volume either more or less 'filled'.

However, since the volume of water envisaged is not that of the displaced water, but rather of the

Floating and Sinking

total quantity of water contained in the receptacle, the relationship between the weight of the body and that of the water remains one between active forces, thus reintroducing a complexity rich in contradictions. The probability that these will appear grows when the air is brought in and also the notion of holes, open or closed, In short, for lack of operational relations sufficiently worked out to cope with the whole body of relationships between weight and volume, the explanation, although vaguely intuited, is not clearly discovered, and a coherent system is not as yet formulated. (Page 35.)

TWO INTERMEDIATE CASES LEADING TO SUB-STAGE IIIA

FRAN (12; 1) does not manage to discover the law, but neither does he accept any of the earlier hypotheses. He classifies correctly the objects presented but hesitates before the aluminium wire. 'Why are you hesitating?—*Because of the lightness, but no, that has no effect.*—Why?—*The lightness has no effect. It depends on the sort of matter: for example the wood can be heavy and it floats.* And for the cover: *I thought of the surface.* The surface plays a rôle? *Maybe, the surface that touches the water, but that doesn't mean anything.*—Thus he discards all his hypotheses without finding a solution.'

FIS (12; 6) also, in the transition phase between Stages II and III, comes close to the solution, saying in reference to a penny that it sinks, '*because it is small, it isn't stretched enough . . . You would have to have something larger to stay at the surface, something of the same weight and which would have a greater extension*'.

SUB-STAGE IIIA

ALA (11; 9). 'Why do you say that this key will

115

sink?—*Because it is heavier than water.* This little key is heavier than that water? (The bucket is pointed out) *I mean the same amount of water would be less heavy than the key.* What do you mean? *You would put them* (metal or water) *in containers which contain the same amount and weigh them'.*

JIM (12; 8) classifies floating or sinking objects according to whether they are *'lighter or heavier than water.* What do you mean? *You would have to have much more water than metal to make up the same weight.* And this cover?—*When you put up the edges, there is air inside: when you put them down, it goes down because the water comes inside, and that makes more weight.*—Why does the wood float?—*Because it's light*—And that little key?— *No, this piece of wood is heavier.*—So?—*If you measure with a key* (with the weight of a key) *you need more wood than lead for the weight of the key.* —What do you mean?—*If you take metal, you need much more wood to make the same weight than metal'.*

MAL (12; 2). *'The silver is heavy, that's why it sinks. —And if you take a tree?—The tree is much heavier, but it is made of wood.*—The silver is heavier than that water? (Bucket)—*No, you take the quantity of water for the size of the object; you take the same amount of water.*—Can you prove that?—*Yes, with that bottle of water. If it were the same quantity of cork it would float because the cork is less heavy than the same quantity of water.*—and again—*A bottle full of water goes to the bottom if it is full because it's completely filled without air, and that bottle stays at the surface if you only fill it halfway'.*" (Page 37.)

Floating and Sinking

Sub-stage IIIB:

Subjects who select cubes of wood, iron and plastic and use them as units to prove their point.

"LAMB (13; 3) correctly classifies the objects that sink; *'I sort of felt that they are all heavier than the water. I compared for the same weight, not for the same volume of water.—Can you give a proof?—Yes I take these two bottles, I weigh them . . . Oh!* (he notices the cubes) *I weigh this plastic cube with water inside and I compare this volume of water to the wooden cube. You always have to compare a volume to the same volume of water.—And with this wooden ball?—By calculation.—But otherwise?— Oh yes, you set the water level* (in the bucket); *you put the ball in and let out enough water to maintain the original level.—Then what do you compare?—The weight of the water let out and the weight of the ball'.*

WUR (14; 4). *'I take a wooden cube and a plastic cube that I fill with water. I weigh them, and the difference can be seen on the scale according to whether an object is heavier or lighter than water'.*" (Page 44.)

Most people have probably had, the experience of reading a particular book or poem in childhood which they remember with enjoyment, feeling it to have been fully appreciated and understood at the time, yet on re-reading the same book or poem when adult, a new light is shed on its contents, and so much richer understanding comes that one wonders how one ever thought one knew it previously. Similarly with people, a knowledge of friends grows and is enriched with the years, yet at any one time we usually feel we know them rather well. So it seems to be with natural

phenomena, we need to live and re-live our activities
with the same materials and objects in new situations
continually working over the ground we know in
order to extend our knowledge.

Young children will make their own opportunities
for collecting basic information about the elements
and qualities of the world, but unless there is opportunity and stimulus at school for them to question
and try to explain what they are observing, their experiences can remain always a matter of enjoyable
play, satisfying immediate interests instead of leading *in addition* to an increase in intellectual understanding about the world and facility in thinking
scientifically, mathematically and logically. Participation by adults is particularly essential at the adolescent stage when children are learning to hypothesize
and test their ideas in scientifically systematic ways.
They need help in clarifying and organizing their
thinking into viable categories which in their turn
lead to further knowledge.

Piaget and Inhelder in this book have taken their in-
vestigations into children's thinking right up to the
adolescent stage. They are particularly concerned to
show the development in the use of hypothetical
reasoning which they maintain reaches its peak
about the ages of fourteen or fifteen. They do this by
setting children of different ages problems drawn
from elementary physics and chemistry. The discovery
of Archimedes' Law has been described above; other
topics investigated are the laws governing angles of
incidence and reflection (any schoolboy with a knowledge of billiards will be able to explain and demonstrate this to the uninitiated): factors controlling the

frequency of the oscillations of a pendulum: motion on a horizontal plane: equilibrium in the hydraulic press and ￼in the balance and the projection of shadows.

The translators in their introduction warn readers not to be turned away by the sight of logical symbols in the book. The results of the experiments are analysed in terms of symbolic logic and this is difficult to understand and relate to the development of thought processes without previous knowledge of this particular logical framework. However, the value of the book to teachers is not likely to lie in this theoretical aspect, it is more likely to be illuminating in the wealth of empirical material recorded from extensive experimental situations.

VII

MORAL JUDGMENT

[Extracts from: *'The Moral Judgment of the Child'* by
Jean Piaget (Routledge and Kegan Paul), 1932]

IN THE FOREWORD to this book Piaget explains his
purpose which is to investigate the growth of moral
judgment in children. He does not merely seek to
examine their moral behaviour or sentiments, but to
try to establish the degree to which children at any
given age and stage can reason 'morally' so that we
may know the framework within which we must
operate when we seek to help them to develop the
moral standards acceptable to our society.

The first two chapters are concerned with children's respect for rules, first in games and then in con-
duct generally, and in the third chapter, from which
the extracts are taken, Piaget is examining the growth
of the notion of justice, how it arises in the child, how
it changes at different ages and what influences it.

His conclusion was that 'the sense of justice though
naturally capable of being re-inforced by the precepts
and the practical examples of the adult is largely independent of these influences and requires nothing

more for its development than the mutual respect and
solidarity which holds among children themselves. It
is often at the expense of the adult and not because
of him that the notions of just and unjust find their
way into the youthful mind. In contrast to a given
rule, which from the first has been imposed on the
child from outside and which for many years he has
failed to understand, such as the rule of not telling
lies, the rule of justice is a sort of immanent condition
of social relationships or a law governing their equilibrium. As the solidarity between children grows we
shall find this notion of justice emerging in almost
complete autonomy'.

This conclusion comes at the end of a most detailed
analysis of children's ideas on punishment. Piaget
began by saying to children, 'Are the punishments
given to children always very fair, or are some fairer
than others?''. He went on to tell them stories of small
misdeeds and discussed with them the punishments
they thought suitable. His judgment as to the level
they had reached in their concept of justice was made
on the basis of the punishments they chose and the
reason they gave for choosing them.

We have, of course, in any such investigation to be
on our guard against the likelihood that children are
saying what they think we are expecting them to say.
Piaget's method of questioning is designed to mini-
mise this danger, but it is, nevertheless, there.

In this extract, a very small part of the whole, two
alternative punishments for the same misdeed are
described, one a severe expiatory one and the other an
explanation and an appeal to reciprocity. They were
asked their ideas on the punishments as such and in

which of the two cases they thought a relapse more likely to recur.

"STORY 1A. 'A boy was playing in his room, while his daddy was working in town. After a little while the boy thought he would like to draw. But he had no paper. Then he remembered that there was some lovely white sheets of paper in one of the drawers of his father's desk. So he went quite quietly to look for them. He found them and took them away. When the father came home he found that his desk was untidy and finally discovered that someone had stolen his paper. He went straight into the boy's room, and there he saw the floor covered with sheets of paper that were all scribbled over with coloured chalk. Then the father was very angry and gave his boy a good whipping'.

B. 'Now I shall tell you a story that is nearly the same, but not quite (the story is repeated shortly, except for the last sentence). Only it ends up differently. The father did not punish him. He just explained to him that it wasn't right. He said 'When you're not at home, when you've gone to school, if I were to go and take your toys, you wouldn't like it. 'So when I'm not there you mustn't go and take my paper either. It is not nice for me. It isn't right to do that'.

Now a few days later these two boys were each of them playing in their garden. The boy who had been punished was in his garden, and the one who had not been punished was playing in his garden. And then each of them found a pencil. It was their fathers' pencil. Then each of them remembered that his father had said that he had lost his pencil in the street and that it was a pity because he wouldn't be able to find it again. So then they thought that if

they were able to steal the pencil, no one would ever know, and there would be no punishment.
'Well now, one of the boys kept the pencil for himself, and the other took it back to his father. Guess which one took it back—the one who had been well punished for having taken the paper or the one who was only talked to?'

* * *

QUIN (6). Repeats story correctly: 'Which one brought the pencil?—*The one who was punished.*—Then what happened, did he do it again or not?—*Not again*—And the one his father didn't punish?—*He stole again.*—If you had been the daddy, when they stole the papers, would you have punished them or explained?—*Punished*—Which is the fairest?—*To punish.* Which is the nicest daddy, the one who punishes or the one who explains?—*The one who explains.*—Which one is the fairest, the one who etc.?—*The one who punishes.*—If you had been the boy, which would you have thought was fairest, to be punished or to have things explained to you?—*Explaining.*—Supposing it had been explained to you, would you have done it again?—*No*—And if you had been punished?—*No. I wouldn't have either*—Which of the two boys didn't do it again?—*The one who was punished.*—What is the good of punishing?—*Because you're a bad boy'* . . .
SCHMEI (7). Story I. 'Guess what the boy who had been punished by his father did.—*He gave it back, because he was afraid his father would scold him again*—And the other one?—*He kept it, he knew his father* (thought he) *had lost it out of doors.*—Which of the two fathers was the most fair?—*The one who punished him properly.*—Which of the two fathers was the most of a sport?—*The one who didn't scold, the one who explained*—Which of the

two boys loved his father best?—*The one whose father was a sport.*—Which boy was the nicest to his father?—*The one who gave the pencil back to his father.*—Was that the one who had been punished, or not punished?—*Punished'.*

Bol (8). Story I. 'Which one gave it back, the.one who was punished or the one who was not?—*The one who was punished.*—What did he think?—*He thought, I don't want to be punished again*—And what did the other one think?—*He thought, 'As I wasn't punished before, I won't be punished this time.*—Which of the two fathers was the most fair? —*The one who punished*—If you had been the father would you have punished him?—*I would have*—Would you have whipped him?—*I would have put him to bed*—Which of the two fathers was most of a sport?—*The one who didn't punish*— Which of the two boys was the nicest?—*The one who was punished*—Which one was the nicest?— the one whose father was fair or the one whose father was a sport?—*The one whose father was fair.*— Supposing you had stolen something would you rather they punished you or explained things to you?—*Punish me*—Should one be punished?— *Yes*—Then the more one is punished the better it is?—*It makes you better'.*

Here finally, is an intermediate case which is interesting as showing a weakening of the preceding beliefs.

Far (8). 'Which one gave it back?—*The one who was punished.*—Why?—*Because he got beaten.*—And the other?—*He kept it because he hadn't been punished.*—Which of the two fathers is the most fair?—*The one who punished.*—Which one was most of a sport?—*The one who didn't beat him*—

Why is he more of a sport?—*Because he explained.*
—Which of the two boys was the nicest?—*The one*
· *who was punished.*—Which of the two fathers was
right?—*The one who didn't beat him.*—Which of
the two fathers would you have given the pencil back
to?—*To the father who didn't punish*—Why?—
Because he was the nicest—If you had been the
father, what would you have done?—*I wouldn't have
punished him, I would have explained*—Why?—
So that he shouldn't steal again—Which of the
fathers was the most fair?—*The one who
punished.*—I've told you a story now you tell me one,
one that really happened, when you were punished.
—*Yes. I ran into the field*—Where?—*Into our field,
in the grass. They hit me,*—And then?—*I didn't do
it again*—And if they hadn't beaten you?—*I would
have have done it again*—Should people always be
punished—*Always when you've been a bad boy'.*

It will be seen how closely all these children, cling
to the traditional view of punishment as morally
necessary qua expiation and educationally useful to
prevent a relapse into evil. The last cases quoted, it
is true, consider it more 'sporting' only to explain
without chastising, but this is neither just nor wise.
Only Far hesitates for a moment towards the middle
of the interrogatory, but the tradition of his fathers
is too strong for him, and he reverts to the customary
morality.

Here, on the contrary, is a different set of opinions,
which may be considered characteristic of a second
type of moral attitude, and up to a certain point, of
a second stage in the social development of the child.
BRIC (8). Story 1. 'What did they do?—*One of them
gave it back, the other kept it*—Which one gave it
back?—*The one who was not punished*—What did

he say to himself?—*That he ought to give it back, because he hadn't been punished.*—And the other one?—*That he ought to keep it*—Why?—*Because he was punished*—The bell rings. Bric goes out for a quarter of an hour's break. We begin again. What were we doing before break?—*Telling a story*—Do you remember what it was?—*Yes about little boys who had stolen. Then afterwards they found a pencil and one of them gave it back and not the other.*—Which one gave it back?—*The one who had not been punished.*—And what did he say to himself? —*That he ought to give it back because his father would be pleased*—And the other one?—*He kept it* —Why?—*Because he didn't want to please his father.*—Which of the two fathers would you like to be?—*The one who explains*—And which of the two children?—*The one who was not punished*—Why? —*Because then he'll know that he mustn't steal* (since it is explained to him)—And if he is punished? What will he do?—*Perhaps he'll try again and then not be punished'.*

SCHU (8). Story 1. The boy who gives back the pencil is the one who has not been punished. 'Why did he give it back?—*Because they explained to him* (about the first theft)—Why?—*Because it's a better way to make him good*—Which of the two fathers is most of a sport?—*The one who explained.*—And which is fairest, explaining or punishing?—*Explaining*— Why did the one who was punished begin again?— And if they had explained to him, would he have begun again?—*No*—Why?—*Because he would have understood*—And wouldn't he have understood that you mustn't steal if he had been punished?—*He wouldn't have understood so well*—Now listen to me carefully. I am going to change the story round a little bit. Let us say that things have been properly explained to both boys. But one of them was also punished, and the other one was only talked to without being punished. Which of the two gave the pencil back later?—*The one who was not punished* —Why?—*Because he had understood things better than the other one*—Why did the other one do it again?—*Because he hadn't understood things quite so well*—Why not?—*Because he was scolded and explained to at the same time*—Does your father not punish you?—*He more often explains*—Do you think it fair that you should be punished?—*No, not fair*—Why?—*Because I can understand things much better when people explain things to me.*—Tell me about once when you were punished.—*Once I was staying with my Granny. I'm never punished at home. But at Granny's I was punished.*—What had you done?—*I had broken a glass*—How were you punished?—*They boxed my ears.*—And does your father not box your ears?—*Hardly ever.*

CLA (9) Story 1. 'Which one gave it back?—*The one that his father explained to*—And what did the other say to himself?—*I may as well take it. Daddy won't see.*—Which of the two fathers was the fairest?— *The one who didn't punish.*—Which is fairest, to punish or not to punish?—*Not to punish*—If you had been the boy, what would you have done?— *I'd have given it back.*—And if you had been punished?—*I'd have given it back all the same.*— Which boy was nicest to his father?—*The one who gave back the pencil.*—But ordinarily, everyday, which one is nicest to his father, the one who is punished often, or the one who is not.—*The one that you explain things to.*—Why?—*Because you don't do it again*—Which is best, to explain and then punish, or to explain and then forgive?—*To explain and then forgive'.*" (Pages 217-8.)

One can see in this extract the truth of Piaget's claim that there is 'a sort of law of evolution in the moral development of a child' (Page 225), from ideas of expiation to those of reciprocity. The genesis of the ideas of expiation might seem to be in the child's natural vindictiveness, a hurt for a hurt, but Piaget believes that it is 'fashioned primarily by adult constraint'. 'Respect for the adult diminishes in favour of equality and reciprocity between children . . . and therefore the idea of expiation gradually loses its power', and the idea of reciprocity takes its place. Children gradually come to see that retribution, in the form of the infliction of 'equal' suffering is ineffective in altering behaviour and that it can only be justified as a measure to 'make the offender realise in what way he has broken the bond of solidarity'. The law of reciprocity, involving as it does an attempt to put oneself in another's place, tends towards a morality of forgiveness and understanding.

What are the implications of this for the teacher?

One point emerges clearly—that children need freedom to make mistakes so that they may see the results of their own small injustices as well as those of others. They need to be in situations safe enough for them to be relatively free of adult interference in this social experimenting because only so can they bring the situation to its own close. After some poignant experience of this kind the youngest children often need to have their energies and attention directed elsewhere, but for junior and secondary school children, it is often profitable to discuss what has happened and clarify with them some of the social implications. It is thus possible to foster the idea of consideration for other people, at first on the grounds that this is the kind of thing one likes oneself. A certain amount of retributive behaviour, however, in young children must be tolerated since it is only through experience of this that we can come to the next stage of thinking and feeling.

Children, then, in general will have different attitudes to punishment in the nursery and infants schools from those they have attained by junior school age. A teacher needs a sliding scale, as it were, of attitudes herself. In general, in the younger ages children are only groping towards the idea of reciprocity with many regressions. They must be given ample opportunity in real social experience to develop this, and the teacher must have flexible ideas about the amount of influence she should exert. It would seem helpful when taking any necessary action to verbalise the reasons in the simplest possible terms setting up the idea that there are reasons for behaviour and that it is something which should be *considered.* Most parents and teachers want their children to acquire the habit of apologising for mistakes and shortcomings but it is fatally easy to form shallow verbal habits without any roots. It is possible to develop a habit of apologising prettily and feeling that that is all that is required, and that the original offence is somehow neutralised by this. If the habit of saying "I'm sorry" is insisted on too early or is not accompanied by some understanding or realisation of the offence it can become very debased coinage indeed.

Generalised discussion of moral issues is not often appropriate in the infants school, but from about 7 onwards, provided an actual occasion gives rise to it, such discussion may help the children to clarify their ideas.

A study of children's ideas on punishment leads one to re-think the whole question of the rules and regulations in school. The planning of the school and classroom must be such that the children's participation in it leads them to think in terms of the solution of problems rather than obedience or, more commonly perhaps, disobedience. (It is a curious fact that by far the greater number of children when asked as in the Binet vocabulary test, to define 'obedience', in fact describe disobedience. Could it be that by emphasizing the times when they are disobedient and refraining from mentioning the many 'obediences', we rouse resentment in children which leads to disobedience of the purely 'contrairy' kind as distinct from that which arises from a wish to do something else).

If the adult organises everything himself then it becomes merely a question of the children's conformity to his plan and the children are learning nothing of reciprocity or self command, nor building up the permanent scale of values which frees us from the tyranny of impulsive behaviour. In this connection it is interesting to note that Piaget, in a telling little essay, 'Will and Action' identifies will power with the possession of this permanent scale of values. The power to 'conserve' values is acquired as gradually and by the same means as we come to an understanding of conservation of quantity etc. (see chapter I) and involves a progressive ability to resolve the conflict between giving way to the present urgent impulse and pausing to consider it in the light of what one really wants to do at a deeper level. This involves

'decentration', the ability to remember what pre-
cedes and anticipate what will follow. This ability
can certainly be encouraged by discussion and often
by asking the questions which will provoke consideration.

Children's ideas on moral issues are, too, leading to
much re-thinking about the type of religious education appropriate to each age. This will be solved in
many individual ways, but Piaget has helped us to
realise the framework within which development can
take place. Whatever conclusions we come to about,
for instance, the direct teaching of religion in school,
the sanctions we impose, whether they are in the realm
of "done" or "not done", or more specifically moral
standards, must be considered in the light of what we
know the children are capable of thinking and feeling
if we wish to make our work of permanent value.

Later in the chapter Piaget explores a number of
concepts of great relevance to school life, cheating,
telling tales and so on. The following extracts may
whet the appetite for a further reading of the book
which develops these and other themes into a
coherent philosophy which cannot be conveyed by
quotations.

"To conclude our examination of the various con-
tacts between authority and equality, let us try to
analyse two school situations where the same factors
may come into play: Why should one not cheat at
school? and: Should one 'tell' if it is in the adult's
interest or if the adult has commanded it?

Cheating is a defensive reaction which our educational systems seem to have wantonly called forth in
the pupil. Instead of taking into account the child's

deeper psychological tendencies which urge him to work with others—emulation being in no way opposed to co-operation—our schools condemn the pupil to work in isolation and only make use of emulation to set one individual against another. This purely individualistic system of work, excellent no doubt if the aim of education be to give good marks and prepare the young for examinations, is nothing but a handicap to the formation of reasonable beings and good citizens. Taking the moral point of view only, one of two things is bound to happen. Either competition proves strongest, and each boy will try to curry favour with the master, regardless of his toiling neighbour who then, if he is defeated resorts to cheating. Or else comradeship will win the day and the pupils will combine in organised cheating so as to offer a common resistance to scholastic constraint.

* * *

The result of our enquiry was very definite. It shows a gradual diminution in the preoccupation with authority and a correlative increase in the desire for equal treatment.

Here are examples of answers that appeal to authority.

MON (6½). 'Why must you not copy from your neighbour?—*The master rows us*'.

DEP (6½). '*Teacher punishes us*'.

THE (6½) '*Because it is naughty*'.

MIR (6½). '*It's bad. You get punished*'.

The definition 'It is deceit' is given only by 5% of the children of 8 and 9, and by 10% of those of 10 to 12.

MART (9). '*He shouldn't have copied from his neighbour. He was being deceitful.*—Why must you not copy?—*Because it is deceit.*'

Here are examples of children who appeal to equality.

THE (9; 7). '*You ought to try and find out yourself'. It isn't fair they should both have the same marks. You ought to find out by yourself.*'

WALD (9; 4). '*It's stealing her work from her.*—And if the master doesn't know?—*It's naughty because of the girl beside her.*—Why?—*The girl beside her might have got it right* (got a good mark) *and her place is taken away'.*

Finally, let us quote a child to whom cheating is something perfectly natural and in whose case the solidarity between children is clearly stronger than the desire for competition.

CAMP (11; 10). 'What do you think about cheating? —*For those who can't learn they ought to be allowed to have just a little look, but for those who can learn ·it isn't fair.*—A child copied his friend's sum. Was it fair?—*He ought not to have copied it. But if he was not clever it was more or less all right for him to do it'.*

This last attitude seems to be rather the exception among the children we examined. But no doubt many others thought the same without having the courage to say so.

If the letter only be considered in the answers appealing to equality it might seem that competition was stronger in children than solidarity. But this is so only in appearance. In reality, equality grows with solidarity. This will appear from the study of one more question which we shall now analyse in order to obtain additional information on the conflicts between adult authority and equality or solidarity between children. We mean the question of "Telling tales".

The contempt which every school child feels for tell-tales or sneaks (Fr. "mouchards", "cafards")—the child's language is significant in itself—and the spontaneous judgment which is pronounced upon them are sufficient to show that this is a fundamental point in the ethics of childhood. Is it right to break the solidarity that holds between children in favour of adult authority? Any adult with a spark of generosity in him will answer that it is not. But there are exceptions. There are masters and parents so utterly devoid of pedagogic sense as to encourage the child to tell tales.

In such cases should one obey the adult or respect the law of solidarity? We put the question by laying the following story to the charge of a father whom we removed to a great distance both in space and time. (Page 285.)

"Once, long ago, and in a place very far away from here, there was a father who had two sons. One was very good and obedient. The other was a good sort but he often did silly things. One day the father goes off on a journey and says to the first son, 'You must watch carefully to see what your brother does, and when I come back you shall tell me'. The father goes away and the brother goes and does something silly. When the father comes back he asks the first boy to tell him everything. What ought the boy to do?"

Here again the result was perfectly clear. The great majority of the little ones (nearly nine-tenths of those between 6 and 7) are of the opinion that the father should be told everything. The majority of the older ones (over 8) think that nothing should be told, and some even go so far as to prefer a lie to the betrayal of a brother.

Here are examples of the different attitudes

adopted, beginning with that of a complete submission to authority.

WAL (6). 'What should be have said?—*That he* (the other) *had been naughty*—Was it fair to say that or not?—*Fair*—I know a little boy in the same story who said to his father: "Look here, it's not my business what my brother has done, ask him himself." Was he right to say this to his father?— *Wasn't right*—Why?—*He ought to have told*— Have you got a brother?—*Yes*—Then we'll pretend that you have made a blot on your copy book at school. Your brother comes home and says "I say, Eric made a blot". Was it right of him to say this?— *He was right*—Do you know what a tell-tale is?— *It's telling what he* (the other) *has done.* Is it telling tales if your brother says that you made a blot?— *Yes*—And in my story?—*It's not telling tales.*— Why?—Because the father had asked him'.

CONST (7). G. '*He ought to have told the father had asked him to.*—Do you know what telling tales is?— *It's telling things*—Was it telling tales or not?—*It was telling tales.*—Have you any sisters?—*Yes, one. She is eleven.*—Does she tell tales about what you do?—*Yes*—Tell me about once when she did it. Who did she tell tales to?—*To mother*—Tell me about it?—*I didn't dare to go out. And I did go all the same.*—Was it nice to tell tales about that or not?— *Nice*—Was she right to tell about it or not?—*She was right*'.

SCHMA (8). '*He ought to have told.*—Was it fair or not?—*Fair*—Once he said that it wasn't his business. —*That was not fair, because his father had said he was to tell.*—Was he telling tales?—*Just then he ought to tell because his father had asked him, but other times he ought not to tell because he hadn't been asked*'.

In (9). '*He ought to have told.*—I am going to tell you three stories: In the first, the boy did tell; in the second, he told the father to ask the brother himself; and in the third, he said that his brother hadn't done anything. Which was the best?—*The first.*—Why?—*Because he told what he* (the brother) *had done, as his father had asked him to.*—Which way was the nicest?—*The first.*—And the fairest?—*The first one too.*—Do you know what telling tales is?—*Telling what someone else has done.*—And here?—*He didn't tell tales, he did what he was told*'.

Here are cases of children who are opposed to telling tales.

Tehu (10; 6). '*I wouldn't have told the father because it was telling tales. I would have said 'He's been good'.*—But if it isn't true?—*I would have said 'he's been good'.*—One child said, 'It's not my business. Ask him himself'. Was that right?—*I can't say that, it's not my business. I would have said he had been good*'.

La (7½). 'What do you think about it?—*I wouldn't have told because the father would have spanked him.*—You would have said nothing?—*No. I'd have said he hadn't done anything silly*'.

Fal (8). 'Should he have told?—*No, because that's telling tales.*—But the father had asked him to.—*He should have said nothing. Have said he'd been nice and good.*—Was it better to say nothing, not to answer, or to say that he'd been nice and good?—*Say he'd been nice and good*'.

Bra (9). '*It rotten of him the one who went and told tales.*—But the father had asked him to. What should he have done?—*Not told tales*'.

Mcha (10). '*He should have said that he hadn't done anything.*—But the brother had played with his father's bicycle and burst one of the tyres. The father wouldn't be able to bicycle to his office the next day and would be late.—*All the same he shouldn't have told.* (Then after some hesitation)—*He ought to tell so that he could put things right at once'.*

Here finally, are two examples of subjects who hesitate. They are, as usual, the most illuminating, because they reveal the nature of the contradictory motives at the back of each of the two views of the matter.

ROB (9). *'I don't know.*—Should the boy have told? —*In a way it was fair, because the father had said so* (asked for it).—Then what should be done?—*He might have told the father a lie because* (otherwise) *it would have been telling tales. But he was bound to tell.*—Which was most of a sport, the one who told what the brother had done, or the one who told a lie?—*The one who didn't tell tales*—And which would have been nicest?—*The one who hadn't told tales.*—Which would have been the most fair?—*The one who told because his father had said he must'.*

WA (10; 3). *'He was quite right, because his father had told him to tell him* (a pause, during which he hesitates).—Are you sure, or were you hesitating?— *I was hesitating.*—Why?—*Because I was thinking that he might also say nothing, so that his brother shouldn't be punished.*—It's hard isn't it?—*Yes*— Then which one do you think is the most of a sport? —*The one who said nothing*—Then what would be the best thing to do?—*It would be best for him to say nothing.*—What would he have said?—*That he had been good'.*

The mechanism of these judgments is clear, on the one hand there is law and authority: since you are asked to tell tales, it is fair to tell tales. On the other, there is the solidarity between children; it is wrong to betray an equal for the benefit of an adult, or at any rate it is illegitimate to interfere in your neighbour's business. The first attitude predominates among the younger children and is related to all the manifestations of respect for the adult which we studied before. The second prevails among the older children for reasons which have also been elucidated by all that has gone before. This second attitude is sometimes so strong that it leads the subject to justify lying as a means of defending a friend. This interrogatory shows, even better than our previous results, the contrast of the two moralities—that of authority and that of equalitarian solidarity.

The conclusion to be drawn from the above facts would therefore seem to be the following. Equalitarian justice develops with age at the expense of submission to adult authority, and in correlation with solidarity between children. Equalitarianism would therefore seem to come from the habits of reciprocity peculiar to mutual respect rather than from the mechanism of duties that is founded upon unilateral respect". (Page 285.)

A study of the group of extracts on cheating leads us to reflect sadly on how often we have ourselves provided the source of children's difficulties, and indeed our own. We give them so many contradictory ideas that they must become confused. We urge co-operation and helpfulness, but at the same time set up individualistic competitiveness by means of stars, marks, place in class etc., and (arbitrarily as it must seem to the children) label some kinds of help to others 'good' and some 'cheating'. In the classroom where children are pursuing their work at their own level and rate, with purposes which they have made their own, cheating, as such, cannot appear. It would be pointless and, in the writer's experience, has never taken place. It is only when the same standard of correctness in some externally imposed exercise is expected from all that there seems any point in cheating, not so much to gain the praise of the teacher, as a rule, as simply to avoid censure on humiliation.

Again in connection with 'telling tales' we are not, perhaps (from the children's point of view) consistent. Every busy teacher at sometime has rebuked a child who has come forward with some long story of what this or that one has done, by saying, "Don't tell tales", yet, after an incident which is important from an adult point of view, we indeed ask first that someone should 'own up', but if that fails, that anyone who knows anything about the incident should help us find out what has happened.

What we want, of course, is to help the children to build up moral judgment in this respect; the power to discriminate between those things which adults must know for the safety of the community and those things which the solidarity and loyalty of children to each other demand that they should keep to themselves. Further, we hope to expand this concept of solidarity beyond the 'not telling' stage, so that it excludes in later life the breaking of confidences or the spreading of malicious gossip.

Any lover of children must be struck on reading 'Moral Judgment' with the immense seriousness with which children's ideas have been analysed and by the skill and sensitivity of the questioning. We are reminded over and over again of the great expansion of our knowledge of children that can come from asking the right question with a real wish to hear the children's answers. Piaget says of this book in his foreword 'It is my sincere hope that it may supply a scaffolding which those living with children and observing their spontaneous reactions can use in erecting the actual edifice. In a sense, child morality throws light on adult morality. If we want to form men and women nothing will fit us so well for the task as to study the laws that govern their formation'.

VIII

BEHAVIOUR OF BABIES

[Extracts from: *'The Origin of Intelligence in the Child'* by Jean Piaget (Routledge and Kegan Paul), 1953. *'The Construction of Reality in the Child'* by Jean Piaget (Routledge and Kegan Paul), 1954]

IT MIGHT BE APPROPRIATE to emphasize at this point that the underlying implication of Piaget's work on the very young children is that to understand children at any point in their lives involves a knowledge of their total history. It has long been recognized in connection with maladjusted children, where a knowledge of their life history is basic to the attempt to bring about their adjustment, but it is not so readily seen in connection with normal intellectual development. The genesis of children's ideas about life, the stage they have reached in their conception of the world and moreover the next step they will take is necessary information for a teacher at every stage in school life.

Every teacher does a certain amount of remedial work every day in the sense that he is required to take part in clearing up misconceptions formed in previous experience and if he is unaware of the stages by which thinking is developed he is doomed to much time-wasting trial and error.

In these two books (and in one other, *Play, Dreams and Imitation*), Piaget is concerned with the beginnings of mental life. In the first, he shows the progressive development of what he calls 'sensori-motor schemata' and the mechanism of adaptation through 'assimilation' and 'accommodation'. It is, he says, on the concrete plane of *action* that infancy makes its intelligence most manifest until the age of 7 or 8. The sensori-motor schemata (repeatable generalized patterns of behaviour that can be applied to different objects in different contexts, e.g., following with the eyes, turning, shaking etc.) thus set up are the first forms of thought and expression.

Mental life, he says, consists of a process of assimilation, by which he means the incorporation of experience into schemata due to one's own activity and a process of accommodation by which these schemata are continually modified to some extent in response to fresh data. Adaptation to one's environment involves attaining progressive states of equilibrium between assimilation and accommodation. The following extract comes late in *The Origin of Intelligence in the Child*, as the sixth stage in the development of mental life in the child of 0–2 years and is described by Piaget as 'characterizing systematic intelligence'.

EXTRACT FROM CHAPTER VI—THE INVENTION OF
NEW MEANS THROUGH MENTAL COMBINATIONS

Observation 180: 1: 4 LUCIENNE. "I put the watch chain inside an empty matchbox, then close the box leaving an opening of 10 mm. Lucienne begins by turning the whole thing over, then tries to grasp the chain through the opening. Not succeeding, she simply puts her index finger into the slit and so succeeds in getting out a small fragment of the chain; she then pulls it until she has completely solved the problem.

Here begins the experiment which we want to emphasize. I put the chain back into the box and reduce the opening to 3 mm. It is understood that Lucienne is not aware of the functioning of the open- and closing of the matchbox and has not seen me prepare the experiment. She only possesses the two preceding schemata: turning the box over in order to empty it of its contents, and sliding her finger into the slit to make the chain come out. It is, of course, this last procedure that she tries first: she puts her finger inside and gropes to reach the chain, but fails completely. A pause follows during which Lucienne manifests a very curious reaction bearing witness not only to the fact that she tries to think out the situation and to represent to herself through mental combination the operations to be performed, but also to the rôle played by imitation in the genesis of representations. Lucienne mimics the widening of the slit.

She looks at the slit with great attentions; then, several times in succession, she opens and shuts her mouth, at first slightly, then wider and wider! Apparently Lucienne understands the existence of a cavity subjacent to the slit and wishes to enlarge that cavity. The attempt at representation which she thus furnishes is expressed plastically, that is to say, due to inability to think out the situation in words or clear visual images she uses a simple motor indication as "signifier" or symbol. Now, as the motor reaction which presents itself for filling this rôle is none other than imitation, that is to say, representation by acting out, which doubtless earlier than any mental image, makes it possible not only to indicate the details of spectacles actually seen, but also to evoke and reproduce them at will. Lucienne, by opening her mouth thus expresses, or even reflects her desire to enlarge the opening of the box. This schema of imitation, with which she is familiar, constitutes for her the means of thinking out the situation. There is doubtless added to it an element of magic—phenomenalistic causality or efficacy. Just as she often uses imitation to act upon persons and make them reproduce their interesting gestures, so also it is probable that the act of opening her mouth in front of the slit to be enlarged implies some underlying idea of efficacy.

Immediately after this phase of plastic reflection, Lucienne unhesitatingly puts her finger in the slit and, instead of trying as before to reach the chain, she pulls so as to enlarge the opening. She succeeds and grasps the chain.

During the following attempts (the slit always being 3 mm wide), the same procedure is immediately rediscovered. On the other hand, Lucienne is incapable of opening the box when it is completely closed. She gropes, throws the box on the floor, etc., but fails". (Page 337.)

In this incident the child finds herself in a situation which is new to her. She tries strategies that have worked before but to no avail. Then, by what appears to be a sudden insight, she invents the means of solving her problem. In reality the schemata she already possesses have combined in a new way so that she perceives the solution by the evocation of absent objects. We can see that she is 'recalling' these by the opening and shutting movement of her mouth.

In the second book, *The Construction of Reality in the Child,* Piaget is making a detailed study of a child's mental functioning during the first 18 months of life in a rather different way: in terms of his gradual acquisition of the concepts of objects, causality, space and time. This he sees as the natural outcome of sensori-motor intelligence at work in an environment that supplies the neecssary stimuli.

In the first chapter, from which the following extract is taken he describes how children develop the idea of the permanence of an object. This he shows as a complex construction in six stages. During the first two the child shows recognition of objects (including persons) but no behaviour related to vanished objects which would indicate that he recognizes their permanence. In the third stage between three and six months of age a child begins to grasp what he sees with his hands, and brings before his eyes the objects he touches, but he does not show active search for vanished objects. Some early beginnings in this are shown in the following extract:

(Page 14/15).

"Obs. 6. Laurent's reaction to falling objects still seems to be non-existent at 0; 5 (24): he does not follow with his eyes any of the objects which I drop in front of him.

At 0; 5 (26), on the other hand, Laurent searches in front of him for a paper ball which I drop above his coverlet. He immediately looks at the coverlet after the third attempt but only in front of him, that is, where he has just grasped the ball. When I drop the object outside the bassinet Laurent does not look for it (except around my empty hand while it remains up in the air).

At 0; 5 (30) no reaction to the fall of a box of matches. The same is true at 0; 6 (0), but then, when he drops the box himself he searches for it next to him with his eyes (he is lying down).

At 0; 6 (3) Laurent, lying down, holds in his hand a box 5 centimetres in diameter. When it escapes him he looks for it in the right direction (beside him). I then grasp the box and drop it myself, vertically and too fast for him to be able to follow the trajectory. His eyes search for it at once on the sofa on which he is lying. I manage to eliminate any sound or shock and I perform the experiment at his right and at his left; the result is always positive.

At 0; 6 (7) he holds an empty match box in his hand. When it falls his eyes search for it even if they have not followed the beginning of the fall; he turns his head in order to see it on the sheet. Same reaction at 0; 6 (9) with a rattle, but this time he has watched the initial movement of the object. The same is true at 0; 6 (16) when his eyes have followed the beginning of the fall, at 0; 6 (20) etc. etc.

At 0; 7 (29) he searches on the floor for everything I drop above him, if he has in the least perceived the beginning of the movement of falling. At 0; 8 (1) he searches on the floor for a toy which I held in my hand and which I have just let drop without his knowledge. Not finding it, his eyes return to my hand which he examines at length, and then he again searches on the floor".

The permanence of the object remains related to

the child's action in following it with his eyes, and later in grasping it. He learns to follow with his hand objects which escape him and it is thus his own behaviour which endows these objects with the first beginnings of permanence. The following extracts are taken at intervals from the long series of steps by which permanence is at length established. (Page 14-15.)

"OBS 13. At 0; 8 (20) Jacqueline takes possession of my watch which I offer her while holding the chain in my hand. She examines the watch with great interest, feels it, turns it over, says 'apff' etc. I pull the chain; she feels a resistance and holds it back with force, but ends by letting it go. As she is lying down she does not try to look but holds out her arm, catches the watch again and brings it before her eyes.

I recommence the game; she laughs at the resistance of the watch and still searches without looking. If I pull the object progressively (a little farther each time she has caught it) she searches farther and farther, handling and pulling everything that she encounters. If I pull it back abruptly, she is content to explore the place where the watch departed touching her bib, her sheet, etc.

But this permanence is solely the function of prehension. If, before her eyes, I hide the watch behind my hand, behind the quilt, etc., she does not react and forgets everything immediately; in the absence of tactile factors visual images seem to melt into each other without substance. As soon as I replace the watch in Jacqueline's hands and pull it back she searches for it again, however.

(Page 28) Obs; 21. At 0; 5 (8) Laurent looks at my hand whose movement he imitates. I am hiding be-

hind his bassinet hood. Several times Laurent obviously tries to see me, his gaze leaving my hand and
rising along my arm to the point where my arm
seems to issue from the hood; he stares at this point
and seems to search for me all around it.

At 0; 5 (25) Laurent shakes himself when I place a
newspaper partly on the edge of his bassinet hood
and partly on the string which connects the hood to
the handle. If he sees a very small portion of the
newspaper he will react in the same way. I observe
several times in succession that he looks behind him
toward the place where the rest of the newspaper is,
as though he is expected to see all of it appear.

At 0; 6 (17) I offer the child a pencil, and at the
moment he is getting ready to grasp it I lower it
gradually behind a horizontal screen. At the first
attempt he withdraws his hand while he still sees one
centimeter of the pencil; he looks at this extremity
with curiosity, without seeming to understand. When
I raise the pencil one to two centimeters he grasps it
at once. Second attempt: I lower the pencil so as to
let about two centimeters of it show. Laurent again
withdraws his outstretched hand. When three to
four centimeters of pencil show he grasps it. Same reactions in a series of sequential attempts; it therefore
seems that the child acknowledges the entireness—
at least virtual—of the pencil when he sees three or
more centimeters of it and believes it is impaired
when he sees only one or two centimeters of it. When
the pencil is entirely hidden, Laurent of course no
longer reacts and even stops looking at the screen.

Obs 22 At 0; 8 (15) Lucienne looks at a celluloid
stork which I have just taken away from her and
which I cover with a cloth. She does not attempt to
raise the cloth to get hold of the toy. . . . But when
a part of the stork appears outside the cloth,

Lucienne immediately grasps this bit as though she recognized the whole animal.

The proof that this involves a reconstruction of the whole is that not every partial presentation is equally propitious. The head or tail immediately gives rise to a search; Lucienne removes the cloth in order to extricate the animal. But sight of the feet alone arouses great interest without the child making any attempt at grasping; Lucienne seems not to recognise the stork, or at least to consider it as being changed. These facts therefore cannot be interpreted by saying that the child grasps at anything. On the other hand, when Lucienne recognizes the stork by just its head or tail she expects to find a whole; she raises the cloth, straightaway knowing in advance that neither head nor tail is isolated. Hence it is all the more curious that the child remains incapable of raising the screen when the entire animal is hidden; it is the sign that the act of reconstructing a whole from a visible fraction of the thing is psychologically simpler than the act of looking for an object that has completely vanished ...

Obs. 36. At 0; 9 (23) (the day after the last observation made on her related to interrupted prehension), Jacueline reveals a reaction which clearly belongs to those of a later stage ...

We recall that, at 0; 9 (21) and 0; 9 (22) when Jacqueline tries to grasp an object on her lap and I place a screen between her hand and the object, she renounces her attempt unless her fingers have already grazed the object. At 0; 9 (23) placed in the same situation, she pursues her search, provided always that the movement of grasping has already been made before the visual disappearance of the object.

Thus I place an eraser on her lap and hide it with my hand at the moment she stretches out her hand.

Jacqueline's hand is at least five centimeters from
the eraser, and has therefore not yet touched it;
however, she continues to search under my hand until she has been completely successful. It also happens that she has her hand over mine when I hide
the eraser; nevertheless she searches for the latter.
However, if the movement of grasping has not been
made before I hide the eraser, it is not set in motion
after the event.

Obs 37. At 0; 10 (3) I resume the experiment. I
place a small spunge on her lap and hide it with my
hand. Contrary to what took place several days
before, Jacqueline immediately grasps my hand, casts
it aside, then takes possession of the object. This
happens a great many times with any objects at all:
pliers, pipe, etc. Moreover, even if Jacqueline has
made no movement before I hide the objects, she
searches for it once it is hidden.

A moment later I place her parrot under a coverlet; she immediately raises it and searches for the
object.

Same reactions at 0; 10 (6) and the days following.
At 0; 10 (12) she scratches a sheet from the outside
and every time she does so I take my index finger
from under the sheet, which makes her laugh. At a
given moment she scratches but I do not take out my
hand again; then she raises the sheet to look for it. A
moment later, new disappointments; she again raises
the sheet, but as she still does not see my hand,
which I purposely withdraw further, she raises the
sheet still higher until she sees my fingers.

It is therefore very clear that she believes in the
substantial existence of the vanished object, whatever
screen may be placed between it and herself.

Obs 38. At 0; 9 (25). Lucienne, like Jacqueline at
the same age, manifests behaviour patterns which are

similar. Moreover Lucienne's intermediate behaviour patterns are interesting in that they foretell
that which is characteristic of the present stage; the
difficulty in conceiving of sequential positions of the
vanished object.

Lucienne is seated on a cloth. I place under its
edge a familiar rubber doll which she likes to suck
and nibble. Lucienne watches me (I work slowly and
visibly), but she does not react.

Second Attempt. This time I let the doll's feet
emerge; Lucienne grabs them at once and pulls the
doll out from under the blanket.

Third Attempt. I again hide the object completely.
Lucienne pulls the cloth about and raises it as
though she were discovering this new procedure in
the very course of her groping, and perceives an extremity of the doll; she leans forward to see better
and looks at it, much surprised. She does not grasp
it.

Attempts 4 and 5 (the doll is henceforth completely hidden each time): negative reaction.

Sixth Attempt: Lucienne again pulls the cloth
about and makes half the object appear. This time
she again looks at it with great interest and at length,
as though she does not recognize it. Then she grasps
and sucks it. . . .

(Page 51). Obs 40. At 0; 10 (18) Jacqueline is seated
on a mattress without anything to disturb or distract
her (no coverlets, etc). I take her parrot from her
hands and hide it twice in succession under the
mattress, on her left, in A. Both times Jacqueline
looks for the object immediately and grabs it. Then I
take it from her hands and move it very slowly before
her eyes to the corresponding place under her right,
under the mattress, in B. Jacqueline watches this
movement very attentively, but at the moment when

the parrot disappears in B she turns to her left and looks where it was before, in A.

During the next four attempts I hide the parrot in B every time without having first placed it in A. Every time Jacqueline watches me attentively. Nevertheless each time she immediately tries to rediscover the object in A; she turns the mattress over and examines it conscientiously. During the last two attempts, however, the search tapers off.

Sixth Attempt: She no longer searches.

From the end of the eleventh month the reactions are no longer as simple and become of the type we call "residual"....

(Page 53). Obs 44. At 0; 9 (17) just after having discovered a box under a cushion, Laurent is placed on a sofa between a coverlet A on the right and a wool garment B on the left. I place my watch under A; he gently raises the coverlet, perceives part of the object, uncovers it, and grasps it. The same thing happens a second time and a third time but with increasing assiduity. I then place the watch under B; Laurent watches this manoeuvre attentively, but at the moment the watch has disappeared under garment B, he turns back towards the coverlet A and searches for the object under that cover. I again place the watch under garment B, Laurent, whose hand is outstretched, raises the garment at once without turning to A; he finds the watch immediately. I then try a fourth time to put the watch under B, but at the moment when Laurent has both hands in the air; he watches my gesture attentively, then turns and again searches for the watch in A.

We see that with the exception of the experiment at the beginning of which Laurent's hand was already directed toward the screening object B, the child has regularly searched for the object in A, even when he has just seen it disappear under B. (Page 21.)

(Page 67). Obs. 53. At 1; 0 (20) Jacqueline watches me hide my watch under cushion A on her left, then under cushion B on her right; in the latter case she immediately searches in the right place. If I bury the object deep she searches for a long time, then gives up, does not return to A.

At 1; 0 (26) same experiment. At the first attempt Jacqueline searches and finds A where I first put the watch. When I hide it in B Jacqueline does not succeed in finding it there, being unable to raise the cushion altogether. Then she turns around, unnerved, and touches different things including cushion A, but she does not try to turn it over; she *knows* that the watch is no longer under it.

Subsequent attempts: Jacqueline never succeeds in finding the watch in B because I hide it too deep, but neither does she ever try to return to A to see if it is still there; she searches assiduously in B, then gives up.

At 1; 1 (22) new experiments with different objects. The result is always the same.

Obs 54 Laurent, at 0; 11 (22) is seated between two cushions A and B. I hide the watch alternately under each; Laurent constantly searches for the object where it has just disappeared, that is, sometimes in A, sometimes in B, without remaining attached to a privileged position as during the preceding stage.

It is noteworthy that the same day Laurent reveals a very systematic mind in searching for the vanished object. I hide a little box in my hand. He then tries to raise my fingers to reach the object. But, instead of letting him do this and without showing the box, I pass to him with two fingers of the same hand a shoe, a toy, and finally a ribbon; Laurent is not fooled and always returns to the correct hand in spite of its movements, and at last opens it and takes the box. When I take it from him to put it in the other hand, he searches for it there immediately.

At 1; 0 (20) likewise, he searches successively in both my hands for a button I am hiding. Afterwards he tries to see behind me when I make the button roll on the floor (on which I am seated) even though, to fool him, I hold out my two closed hands.

At 1; 1 (8) etc. likewise, he takes note of all the visible displacements of the object.

Obs 54a. Lucienne also at 1; 0 (5) looks for the object only in B and does not return to the initial place, even in the event of continuous failure.

Same observations at 1; 0 (11) etc." (Page 67.)

Chapter I summarised above, has shown how the child has come to construct in his mind a world of objects (which includes himself as an element in it). At first, as we have seen, objects do not exist for the child apart from his own action, and action alone confers on them their quality of constancy. Chapter II demonstrates how his apprehension of space follows the same model. Space, to him is, at first, a property of his own action. Indeed to him there are many spaces only co-ordinated as his actions become so. (See chapters on space).

Chapter III is perhaps the most interesting for teachers. Here again, in a child's conception of causality, we see the same process at work. A child begins to understand causality by himself becoming a cause through his own action. It is one of the chief ways in which he learns to attend to certain stimuli or factors and ignore others in discovering the cause of any phenomenon. But he has also to go on to realise that his parents, and other people are equally causes, through *their* action. These processes are illustrated in the following: —

"Obs 150. Here is an observation made on Jacqueline at 1; 3 (9) in which she does not succeed in finding the cause sought but in the course of which the same attitudes of objectification may be found.

I present the child with a clown whose arms move and activate cymbals as soon as one presses his chest. I put him in motion, then offer him to Jacqueline. She grasps him, looks him all over, evidently trying to understand. Then she tries to move the cymbals directly, each in turn. After this she touches the clown's feet and tries to move them. Same effort with the buttons attached to the chest. She gives up, sighs, and looks at him. I put him in action once more: Jacqueline cries *pou* quite loudly (causality through imitation of the sound) then touches the buttons again. After a new stimulus from me Jacqueline once more shakes the cymbals, crying "pou, tou," etc. (imitation of the totality observed), then she again tries to shake the buttons and gives up the project.

Thus we see that, besides an attempt at direct action (activating the cymbals) and action through the efficacy of imitation, Jacqueline searches on the very body of the clown (feet, buttons, etc.) for the cause of the movement observed.

Obs. 151. Similarly, at the end of his first year Laurent attributes an entirely objectified causality to to objects.

At 1; 0 (0) for example, he takes possession of a new ball which he has just received for his birthday and places it on top of a sloping cushion to let it go and roll by itself. He even tries to make it go by merely placing it on the floor, and, as no movement is produced, he limits himself to a gentle push.

At 1; 0 (9) Laurent is standing near a panel of the open French window against which is the back of a chair. I move the window by pushing the chair slightly with my foot. Laurent, who has not noticed the movement of my foot, is surprised by the sudden displacement of the window and tries to understand it. He moves the window panel against the back of the chair, then gives the chair a little shake to make sure it was the cause of the movement. He is satisfied only after having reproduced the phenomenon exactly. Such a causal sequence is therefore simultaneously objectified and spacialized." (Page 274.)

Obs 156. At 1; 6 (6) Jacqueline watches me as I place a little lamb on top of a quilt and make it run faster and faster toward her (I go "tch, tch, tch" while I make the toy descend and she bursts out laughing). After this I place the lamb on top of the quilt, withdraw my hand, and remain motionless. Jacqueline waits a moment, without trying to act upon the lamb herself. Then when I go "tch, tch, tch" she looks at the animal but seeing it without my hand she immediately looks at my arm, remaining fixed in that position. Jacqueline therefore knows that the the lamb will not put itself in motion but that my hand alone is cause of the movement—this is objectified and specialized causality—and she is expecting to see my hand move in the direction of the object. This is the beginning of representation of causality but, as Jacqueline has just perceived my hand in contact with the lamb, it is still only anticipation based on immediate experience; such behaviour by itself cannot mark the transition from the fifth stage to the sixth.

But the next day, at 1; 6 (7) Jacqueline is examining the arm of an old chair, unfamiliar to her, with an extension leaf used for trays, which I operate from behind. This time Jacqueline has not seen me do this and does not see my arm when I push the leaf. Nevertheless when it stops Jacqueline immediately turns to me, looks at my hand, and definitely shows by her behaviour that she considers me the cause of the object's movement. Hence this involves mental reconstruction of the causes of a perceived effect.

Obs 157. At 1; 6 (8) Jacqueline sits on a bed beside her mother. I am at the foot of the bed on the side opposite Jacqueline, and she neither sees me nor knows I am in the room. I brandish over the bed a cane to which a brush is attached at one end and I swing the whole thing. Jacqueline is very much interested in this sight: she says "cane, cane" and examines the swinging most attentively. At a certain moment she stops looking at the end of the cane and obviously tries to understand. Then she tries to perceive the other end of the cane, and to do so, leans in front of her mother; then behind her, until she has seen me. She expresses no surprise, as though she knew I was the cause of the sight.

A moment later, while Jacqueline is hidden under the covers to distract her attention, I go to the foot of the bed and resume my game. Jacqueline laughs, says "Papa", looks for me in the place she saw me the first time, then tries to find me in the room, while the cane is still moving. She does not think of finding me at the foot of the bed (I am hidden by the footboard), but she has no doubt that I am the cause of the phenomenon.

Obs 159. Lucienne and Laurent have presented

analogous behaviour patterns at the same ages. Here are just two examples.

At 1; 1 (4) Laurent is seated in his carriage and I am on a chair beside him. While reading and without seeming to pay any attention to him, I put my foot under the carriage and move it slowly. Without hesitation Laurent leans over the edge and looks for the cause in the direction of the wheels. As soon as he sees the position of my foot he is satisfied and smiles.

At 1; 4 (4) . . . Laurent tries to open a garden gate but cannot push it forward because it is held back by a piece of furniture. He cannot account either visually or by any sound for the cause that prevents the gate from opening, but after having tried to force it he suddenly seems to understand; he goes around the wall, arrives at the other side of the gate, moves the armchair which holds it firm, and opens it with a triumphant expression." (Page 295.)

Thus the child gradually learns to treat causality as something not merely bound up with his own actions, but also with those of other people. In fact he comes to represent it freely in his mind as essentially a linkage between something done, or happening, and certain further happenings. And he has even begun to see that before an effect can be produced there has to be spatial contact between the action, or means of action, and what is to be acted upon. But he is still liable to slide back at times into overlooking this.

Obs 163. First, here are some of Jacqueline's residual behaviour patterns relating to things and not to people.

At 1; 6 (8) she is seated in a double bed facing a

quilt rolled up to make a hill. I place on top of it a little wooden lamb and strike the bottom of the quilt so that at each shake the lamb comes nearer the child and finally rolls into her hands. Then I put the lamb back on top of the quilt; Jacqueline immediately imitates successfully what she has just learned and makes the lamb roll to her two or three times in succession.

Then I place the lamb on a bedside table at a distance of about one meter from Jacqueline and at the same height as herself but separated from the bed by a space about 80 centimeters wide. Jacqueline strikes the quilt as before, while looking at the lamb and striking harder and harder as though the failure of this procedure were due to the weakness of the blows.

Fifteen minutes later; same behaviour with a fish which she has made fall from the quilt, and which she seems to want to reach by the same procedure after I have put it on the bedside table.

When I put the lamb or fish on the window sill, that is, farther away and a little higher, she looks at it without reacting, but as soon as I put it back on the table, she begins again to strike the quilt.

At 1; 6 (13) five days later, Jacqueline is in the same bed. I take the lamb from her but instead of placing it on the quilt I put it on the table and push it lightly with my fingers. As soon as I stop, Jacqueline strikes the quilt while watching the toy.

At 1; 6 (20) she is in another bed. I put my watch chain on top of the quilt. She immediately strikes the quilt, and the chain slides to her. Jacqueline laughs and does it again. Then I take the object and place it on a chair, one meter from the bed; Jacqueline hits the quilt two or three times but but weakly and without conviction, as though to see if perhaps the procedure would succeed notwithstanding. Then I put the chain on the back of the chair; Jacqueline looks at it but no longer reacts.

Obs. 164. If the foregoing behaviour patterns were elicited by our experimentation, here, on the contrary, is an analogous example of spontaneous behaviour.

At 1; 6 (5) Jacqueline walks into a room and moves a chair whose back touches one of the panels of an open french window. The window stands slightly open and Jacqueline notices the movement imparted to it indirectly. Then she grasps the chair with both hands and shakes it, this time intentionally, while watching the window and the shaking thus produced. Afterward Jacqueline continues her walk in the room without seeming to pay any further attention to the phenomenon. But on knocking against another chair two meters away, she grasps it, shakes it as before and looks at the window. She sees that a wide empty space separates her from the window and that no longer contact exists between it and the new chair; nevertheless, despite failure, for a while she continues to shake the chair while watching the window.

Obs 165. Let us now take up Jacqueline's residual procedures relating to people.

At 1; 9 (28) Jacqueline comes and goes in a dimly lighted room. I am lying on a sofa with a cape over my legs, which are bent. Jacqueline notices the hill thus formed and comes and puts her head on it. I move slightly; she lifts her head abruptly, smiles, puts it back again, and I recommence. When I definitely stop, she shakes her head harder and harder while watching the hill. This movement, evidently designed to make me continue, is not directed at me but at my knees which are covered with a cape.

Jacqueline does not look at my face which is barely visible in the growing darkness and perhaps does not even know that the legs under the cape are mine.

At 1; 10 (16) Jacqueline plays in a room on which I have been in bed since morning, as I am ill. She does not see me and is behind the wood of the bed, my keys in her hand. She encounters the wastepaper basket and strikes its empty bottom with the keys. Then I cry out: 'Oh ...' she starts, then laughs, knowing it is I, and without turning round, starts to strike again. I cry out again, and so on for six.or seven times. Then I pause and look at her without her seeing me. She increases her blows, and, noting failure, withdraws her keys with her right hand, with her left slowly pushes the basket about ten centimeters farther away, as though to adjust it, and begins striking again. I cry out once more, and she bursts out laughing. But I remain silent when she resumes striking. Then the whole manoeuvre is repeated. She increases the blows, withdraws the keys, re-adjusts the basket a few centimeters farther away, and strikes again. Jacqueline thus seems to believe that my cries depend on the way she strikes and the position of the basket, as though they were substantially governed by these factors and not solely by my wish to amuse her. Jacqueline does not try to look at me or to exchange a word with me". (Page 301.)

Here Jacqueline quickly distinguishes those situations in which the lamb will respond to her 'blows' knowing from the beginning the futility of the procedure if the lamb is on the window sill but taking longer to grasp the idea in connection with shorter distance and appearance of contiguity. The last example is not a natural 'cause and effect' one. It is a deliberate attempt by the experimenter to set up a false causal situation. In this it is made clear that contiguity sets up the idea of causal connection and that the child's own repetition or practice of this proves or disapproves the matter. Where there is a functional connection this behaviour confirms the connection, where there is not, the idea dies away. The mere perception of one event occurring after another, does not give understanding of causality and may even give a false idea of it as in Jacqueline's case. Piaget has shown that a true idea is developed from the child's experience of himself as an active agent. This experience can then be represented or internalised and eventually, though not much before the junior school, be generalised into a concept.

To the child 'the initial universe is not a web of causal sequences but a mere collection of events arising in extension of activity itself'. His task, in maturing, is to construct this web of causal sequences bit by bit with some recurring re-construction as his contact with the real world increases and his dependence on fantasy or autistic solutions decreases. Our responsibility in school is to foster that task by the provision of materials for investigation and construction and by conversation about them when we help children to look for and to evaluate causal relationships. This is necessary throughout the school and at each level the full understanding of causal relationships is preceded by appropriate activity. Advances in understanding are commonly preceded by, first, a 'hunch' about a causal connection, and then a 'trying-out' phase, leading either to success which satisfies the child for the time, or a temporary abandonment of the problem and a return to it later. Here we have a clear sequence of learning. Children's 'why' questions—where they mean, as they often do, 'What makes . . .?'—are very good lead-ins to this sequence. On the other hand, instruction given in advance of children's own questioning or thinking, and without the opportunity of testing his hunches out, is impermanent and as shallow and liable to misconception as perception itself. If a child's learning has come in response to his own desire to know, and if he has really grasped the process he can, even after a lapse of time when memory of how to tackle the problem has escaped him, reconstruct the method.

This idea is as appropriate in the secondary as in the primary stages. The weakness of much science teaching, for instance, where it consists of observation of the teacher performing an experiment to prove something he has been saying (often something already known), lies in the shallow 'rote knowledge' which results and in which failure of memory can mean total loss, since understanding at any stage is properly grounded only in the wish to find out, and the *active* search for a solution. As time goes on, this will rightly include an increasing element of verbal discussion rather than the mainly physical activity which best holds the interest of the younger children. The point of 'active' lies in the seeking behaviour of the subject.

It is this 'seeking behaviour' which wise educationists try to use to best advantage. The desire to understand arises probably most often in the service of the desire to do or make—to shape parts of the world in accordance with our own desires. It is then that children will accept the 'drudgery' of studying the nature of the material, trying to find out what actions bring about what results, what obstacles have to be overcome, or how to deal with possible interfering factors, and so on.

This goes far beyond the field of casuality proper; the moral is the same for every kind of learning. The whole foundation of a child's knowledge of the world lies in his own actions, which he then internalizes to form the 'stuff' of his thinking. It would seem clear that this is true of learning at all stages and in all areas. Without the opportunity to build on this first hand knowledge, to expand it by analogy with the knowledge of others, to codify and systematise it as suitable stages are reached, it could stay at a primitive level (though even so it would be more genuine and more capable of growth than externally imposed dogma). The teaching of grammar provides a good example of this. If children talk and read they get a working knowledge of language in which words in each part of speech increase proportionately. A short time spent in explaining the different functions of the words and phrases at a mental age of thirteen or fourteen can bring full and complete understanding of elementary grammar. If we begin to teach formal grammar before 'function' is understood as distinct from 'meaning' we get great confusion which turns 'grammar' into a dreaded item on the time-table. Moreover it has now become so emotionally charged that understanding is unreasonably delayed.

The relation between the active will to achieve something and an understanding readiness to accept even 'drudgery' in the service of this comes out in every sort of field. Thus a junior school child, and perhaps a secondary modern one, who wants to be able to speak French, may develop a craze for learning French words and phrases and can enjoy all the efforts he has to make in order to communicate in this foreign tongue. But a rough-and-ready level of practical success may satisfy his ambitions; whilst a grammar school child, who wants to get much further, may see the necessity for studying the structure of the language and willingly submit himself to this. Here again, however, since the analysis of the structure of a language comes late in the development of a language, it would seem logical to put it late in the learning of it.

It is perhaps in connection with physical skills that the operation of the inward will to learn is most readily observable. Boys and girls value physical skills for their own sake and for the sake of their personal standing with others. But whatever the motive, once the real desire to master the skill is present, children will practice assiduously and indeed often to exhaustion, without adult prompting. Similarly the really musical or artistic child is driven to practice by his own wishes. The problem can even become one of two exclusive attention to his special skill to the neglect of other sides of his life.

Young children's learning is really all of this kind before they come to school. It is very difficult indeed to teach them anything they do not want to learn! It cannot be beyond our wit to carry this on fruitfully throughout school life if we remember the degree to which our interests depend on our opportunities. A really rich and stimulating school environment engenders interests which in turn engender the energy to pursue them.

Much boredom and frustration has become connected with too much of school life and some of this has been defended in the name of 'the discipline of subject matter'. The truth is that the discipline of the subject is intrinsic and comes, as it were, from the inside. Anything else is really the discipline of a person on a person via subject matter. The true objection to this is the poor quality of learning that takes place. It does not resemble the true genetic organic growth where one stage grows out of the last, but is ephemeral, shallow-rooted stuff which does not survive beyond the examination hurdle it is designed for, and even worse, may get in the way of true knowledge because of the confusion it has produced.

Time spent on Piaget's books about early childhood, is rewarding for a teacher at any stage since it shows the fundamental *connection* between action and learning and the extent to which true learning is dependent on the activity of the learner. 'Activity' is no fanciful addition to the curriculum to give children more enjoyment (though it does) but the necessary element in all learning skill. Piaget has helped us to understand what we mean by activity, by revealing its rôle in the genesis of mental structure and therefore of 'mind' itself.

CONCLUSION

IT WAS NOT OUR INTENTION to give, or even 'cover', the main theories which Piaget has developed, but perhaps a few words about his much discussed theory of stages of cognitive development may serve as a summing up.

Stage I, from 0 to about 2 years of age, Piaget defines as the sensori-motor stage, in which a child learns to co-ordinate his actions with what he perceives, or with other actions and to use certain elementary schemata, i.e., *ways* of behaving applicable to many different objects (e.g., following with eyes, shaking, rattling, sucking, etc.). During this time he achieves the idea of the permanence of an object even when it is not immediately before him and a first-level understanding of some relationships in space, causality and time. The chapter on 'Infant Behaviour' particularly illustrates this stage and its transition to the next.

Stage 2, from 2 to about 7 years of age, is pre-operational. In it the child learns to represent the world through the medium of signs and symbols i.e., images and words. He constantly re-organizes his picture of the world through his imaginative play, talking, questioning, listening and experimenting. During the last two years of this period he advances towards the stage

Conclusion

of concrete operations. (See 'Knots' and 'Number').

Stage 3, from about 7 to 11 years of age, is the stage of concrete operations i.e., when the child can deal with the properties of the immediately present world gradually building up the ideas of conservation of matter and length in the earlier phases, and weight and volume later and so on (see chapters IV, V, VI). An operation is a means of organising facts already internalised about the real world so that they can be used selectively in the solution of new problems.

Stage 4, reached sometime between 12 to 15 years of age, involves 'formal' as well as concrete operations, i.e., it involves being able to make free use of hypothetical reasoning. During this stage children are learning to attack problems from the angle of all possible combinations and can perform controlled experiments in which they can observe the effect of altering one or more variables at a time. (see chapter VI).

It will readily be seen that these stages merge gradually into each other through many sub-stages and that in fact the earlier stages are absorbed into later thinking. At certain times and with new materials we may need to think *first* in a way usually connected with earlier stages.

The real difficulty in the concept of stages is the apparent contradiction involved in believing at one and the same time in continuity of growth and in *stages* of growth. Piaget explains this by demonstrating that during the formation of a structure of reasoning each new procedure depends on the one a child has previously acquired, but once that structure is formed (e.g. see conservation of quantity Chapter I) it becomes the starting point of a new acquisition and relatively independent of the earlier steps, though inclusive of them.

A difficulty of interpretation has arisen by a too literal gearing of ages and stages. Piaget gives the average ages for the attainment of the stages of thinking of children he tested. He is less concerned with this however, than with the *order* of the stages and the mastery of material within them, which he claims is constant.

He does not look on these as maturational levels or as educational ones but as the result of assimilation and accommodation (see page 164) which in their turn are dependent on the interaction between maturation and experience.

WORKS REFERRED TO

1. Piaget, J., *The Child's Conception of Number (1941).* (Routledge & Kegan Paul, 1952, tr. C. Cattegno and F. M. Hodgson). *Chapter V. Page 103. Dolls and Sticks.* Pages 6, 13, 18, 43, 44, 47, 99, 103, 105, 113.
2. Inhelder, B., Piaget, J. and Szeminska, A., *The Child's Conception of Geometry.* (Routledge & Kegan Paul, 1960, tr. E. A. Lunzer). *Curved and straight sticks.* Pages 92-3, 94, 95.
3. Piaget, J. and Inhelder, B., *The Child's Conception of Space.* (Routledge & Kegan Paul, 1956, tr. F. J. Langdon and J. L. Lunzer). Chapter IV, *The Study of Knots and the Relationship of Surroundings.* Pages 107, 108-9, 112, 113-115, 118-119, 121-122.
4. Chapter VIII. *The Co-ordination of Perspectives.* Pages 210, 218, 219, 227, 236, 240.
5. Chapter XIII. *Systems of Reference and Horizontal and Vertical Co-ordinates.* Pages 378-381, 382, 384, 390, 391, 398-399, 406.
6. Piaget, J. and Inhelder, B., *The Growth of Logical Thinking* (Routledge & Kegan Paul). Chapter II, *The Law of Floating Bodies.* Pages 20, 22, 24, 26, 29, 33, 37, 44.
7. Piaget, J., *The Moral Judgment of the Child* (Routledge & Kegan Paul, 1932, tr. M. Gabain), Chapter III. Pages 217-218, 219-223, 285-294. *Idea of Justice.*

Works Referred to

8. Piaget, J., *The Origins of Intelligence in the Child* (Routledge & Kegan Paul, 1953, tr. M. Cook). *Lucienne and the Match-Box*, Chapter VI, Page 337.
9. Piaget, J., *Construction of Reality in the Child* (Routledge & Kegan Paul, 1954, tr. M. Cook). *Jacqueline and the Lamb*, Chapter III, Pages 14-15, 21, 28-29, 47-48, 51, 53, 67-68, 301.